Billy Wilder, American Film Realist

Billy Wilder,
American Film Realist

by

RICHARD ARMSTRONG

McFarland & Company, Inc., Publishers
Jefferson, North Carolina, and London

All photographs provided by BFI Films: Stills, Posters and Designs.

Library of Congress Cataloguing-in-Publication Data

Armstrong, Richard, 1959–
　　Billy Wilder, American film realist / by Richard Armstrong.
　　　　p.　　cm.
　　Filmography: p.
　　Includes bibliographical references and index.
　　ISBN 0-7864-0821-9 (illustrated case binding : 50# alkaline paper) ∞
　　1. Wilder, Billy, 1906–　— Criticism and interpretation.　I. Title.
PN1998.3.W56A87　　2000
791.43'0233'092 — dc21　　　　　　　　　　　　　　　　　　00-24224

British Library cataloguing data are available

Cover photograph: ©2000 MPTV Media Vault

Manufactured in the United States of America

*McFarland & Company, Inc., Publishers
　Box 611, Jefferson, North Carolina 28640
　　www.mcfarlandpub.com*

Contents

Acknowledgments

Before acknowledging the many individuals who, through their advice, assistance, encouragement and patience, helped bring this book in to land, I must pay particular tribute to a Wilder film by recalling that Charles Lindbergh had to learn how to build a plane before he could learn how to fly the Atlantic. As for myself, I have had to learn how to write *a book* before I could learn how to write *this* book. I hope the lessons were worth it.

First of all, my thanks go to my family, and to Susan Waters for being there during the early tests and during the most crucial stages of the flight. Secondly, I must acknowledge Kevin Harley's perceptive and enthusiastic input during screenings which lasted well into the night. Thanks also to Neil Sinyard and Adrian Turner for allowing me access to hard-to-find Wilder films and for sharing their thoughts with me. Patrick Mulcahy of *Cinema Release* magazine was the first editor to allow me space to try out ideas later refined in the book. Bob Wilson of *Audience* magazine encouraged me to expand them for an American debut, while John Ashbrook put them between the covers of a book. Thanks too are owed my students, in particular May Sinclair, who responded with so much insight to the plight of Bertram Potts and Max Von Mayerling.

And finally my thanks go to all those assistants at the BFI Reading Room who, for many, many hours, have helped me trawl through all those writers whose observations on the films of Billy Wilder have fueled this journey.

Introduction

In his biography *Billy Wilder in Hollywood*, Maurice Zolotow tells a story in which Wilder, newly arrived in America in 1934, is asked by Columbia executive Sam Briskin what nationality he is. "I — I — been — Austrian," Wilder nervously replies. "Billy — what kinda name is that for an Austrian?" Briskin retorts.[1]

Billy Wilder, an Austrian Jew, was born in 1906, the son of Max and Eugenia Wilder. Frau Wilder had lived as a young girl in New York and had grown to love America. She had always dreamed of emigrating, and Samuel (Billy) and his brother Willie were regaled with stories of Coney Island, Buffalo Bill, the elevated trains and the vast blue Atlantic. Legend has it that Wilder was nicknamed after Buffalo Bill, with whom Frau Wilder had been infatuated. These impressions of the New World left their mark on Wilder, and by the mid–1920s he had become infatuated with the feverish strains of the new American dance music and was an able student of the latest steps. Breaking into journalism, Wilder went to Berlin, becoming a hardworking freelancer with extensive knowledge of jazz and American culture.

Even the briefest acquaintance with a handful of Wilder's best films reveals a European who rapidly took to being an "American" in sensibility. But rather than trade in a realistic evocation of Europe, Wilder's films often depict a universe which was merely "European" in flavor. If the New York City of Woody Allen's work remains fresh from film to film because he lives and works there, Wilder's portraits of New York, Cleveland and Los Angeles too contain a startling veracity. Partly because of Wilder's and his cinematographers' striking use of the actual locations, these

1

American portraits owe much to Wilder's feeling for the voices and culture of these cities. By contrast, his "European" locations lack substance, seeming to be backdrops to the action.

Challenging the accusations of cynicism and bad taste leveled at Wilder in the 1960s, Neil Sinyard and Adrian Turner, in their book *Journey Down Sunset Boulevard*, drew attention to Wilder's gentler, more romantic, European sensibility. Their book (now regrettably out of print) is the best study of Wilder's work to date. It is true that his European frolics such as *Sabrina, Love in the Afternoon* and *Avanti* possess a generosity of spirit missing from his harder-edged, more "American" works. But while the Continental romps remain funny and telling in their ways, the Wilder films which for me have remained most powerful and pristine are those which examine what Sinyard and Turner called the "grotesque gracelessness of modern life"[2] as it has been lived in Wilder's adopted country and, now more than ever, in Europe: *Double Indemnity, Sunset Blvd.* and *The Fortune Cookie*.

Wilder was a graduate of the "university" of Paramount, a studio renowned for the Continental look of its product. John Baxter sums it up: Paramount "was the direct antithesis of Metro–Goldwyn–Mayer. Metro, American controlled and financed, expressed a typically American impulse, endorsing the virtues of money, position and honest lust.... Paramount was European in style and approach. Its key directors and technicians were European and many of its stars came, as the filmmakers did, from Germany, where Paramount's sister company, UFA-EFA, provided a recruiting point and proving ground.... If Metro's films had polish, Paramount films had a glow. The best of them seem gilded, luminous, as rich and brocaded as Renaissance tapestry.... Its cameramen were masters in the use of diffusers to spread the light, and in softening it to give the simplest film a characteristic warmth.... At Paramount, the sly sexual comedy and ornate period film came into their own.... Paramount's was the cinema of half-light and suggestion; witty, intelligent, faintly corrupt."[3]

Production manager at Paramount from 1935 was the Berliner Ernst Lubitsch, who had established himself at Warner Bros. in the '20s with a string of witty comedies. Significantly for Wilder, what characterized Lubitsch's working methods was a fastidious attention to the script. With all the studied aplomb of the dialogue tradition which they served, the films which Lubitsch directed and those which Wilder wrote in the '30s are supreme examples of narrative inter-breeding — forged by Europeans of varied stocks, meshing characters and conventions from an assortment of plays, novels, films, reportage and history itself.

Watching a Billy Wilder film is like reading a compelling novel, and the impact of a Wilderian location comes from the deft manner in which it is accounted to his purposes. But if "Jerry's Market" on Melrose Avenue, Los Angeles, contributed poignantly to Wilder's examination of consumerism in *Double Indemnity*, the Brandenberg Gate, resonating with history, is merely a handy trump from a compendium of screenwriting clichés in *One, Two, Three*. In *Love in the Afternoon*, the actual feel and atmosphere of the Eiffel Tower are passed over in favor of its use as a tourist icon. Even the sexual phenomenology of the Lubitschian boudoir confection was, in the Wilder-scripted *Ninotchka*, replaced by "a hard, brightly-lit, cynical comedy with the wisecrack completely in control."[4]

There is a sense in which, as a filmmaker, Wilder, who became a naturalized American in 1939, did not care for Europe as it phenomenally existed. But then Wilder did not have to care about portraying Europe as real experience. He was making films for audiences raised on movies and television. Classical Hollywood audiences were used to depictions of foreign societies which were framed in conventions of representation. If Frenchmen all sounded like Maurice Chevalier, that was as it should be. If Middle-Europe looked like Ruritania that too was fine.

However, by the early '60s, cheap air travel had made Wilder's middle-class audience worldly, and Paramount exotica fraudulent. By the late '60s, his work had become uneven. One reason, it is fair to say, is that his films lacked the spark once produced when his cold eye chronicled American realities.

Billy Wilder's career is a classic example of the emigrant leaving Europe, buying into the American world view, and selling the outlook back in Europe. Indeed, his film of Charles Lindbergh's pathbreaking Atlantic flight, *The Spirit of St. Louis*, can be seen as a meditation upon the process by which Americans make films which make the rest of the world worldly. However, Wilder also perhaps includes a critique of the ethos of mass production which makes this process possible. Lindbergh's (and Wilder's) building a plane specifically to fly the Atlantic could be read as a tribute to the unrepeatable art object, traditionally a European aesthetic ideal.

Turning his back on a shell-pocked Vienna in 1948's *The Emperor Waltz*, Wilder concocted a "fluffy Franz Josef conceit out of the cuisine of Chez Ernst."[5] However, its key line is timely, as the old Emperor tells the American salesman: "You are simpler, you are stronger. Ultimately the world will be yours." In 1945, Europe was liberated by American forces, and in 1948, American dollars were building the Continent's "American" future.

Billy Wilder (left, in sunglasses) on location for *The Spirit of St. Louis*, Warner Bros., 1957.

It is fair to say that Wilder's "European" films are vivid texts on the Americanization of Europe, in terms of both its economic and its aesthetic recasting. It was not Wilder's intention that his 1948 Berlin comedy *A Foreign Affair* should become part of the American propaganda effort to de–Nazify the Germans. Seen today, the film most interestingly essays the evolving screen images of Hollywood stars Jean Arthur and Marlene Dietrich. *A Foreign Affair* is simply a very capable genre comedy. In a letter[6] outlining his findings as Military Government Film Officer to the U.S. Armed Forces in Berlin, Wilder explained how the texture of his dialogue should strike a balance between proselytizing zeal and entertainment, a feat which recalls the imperatives of the seasoned studio hack. One can see how, in its often brilliant dialogue, the "Paramount Sound" simplified and added polish to complex European ethical and political disputes as efficiently as the "Continental look" had packaged its hotels and street corners.

For Wilder, to be making films was to be making fictions. For all the fanfare which announces London's Old Bailey in *Witness for the Prosecution*, a location which Wilder could not use and had to recreate, it becomes the scene for some fine speechmaking by actor Charles Laughton. This artifice is borne out if one sees the courtroom spectators as an audience and the whole affair as an essay on the art of making movies. The reason why *One, Two, Three*, set as the Berlin Wall was going up, seemed crass to Pauline Kael in 1962 is that its manic scenario exploited a situation which had complex political dimensions. With distance, Sinyard and Turner in 1979 read the film as mirroring America's evolution from Virgin Land to Superpower. With greater hindsight, this dynamic screenplay not only simplifies the ragged conflicts of German and American history, but recalls the most manic of '30s Hollywood screwball comedies. As is usual with Wilder, no distracting camerawork or cutting is allowed to stand in the way of dialogue, which cuts its cloth to fit MacNamara's (and Wilder's) myopic odysseys.

If the locations of Wilder's "European" films are invisible, their locutions are far from silent. Wilder cares deeply for the word. It is a treat to close one's eyes and listen to a Wilder film. His grasp of English is consummate, with a feel for the American idiom rare in a Continental European. These are American voices. His use of Yiddish in the characterizations of Dr. Dreyfuss and his wife in *The Apartment* evokes less the *shtetls* of Sholem Aleichem than the tenements of Malamud. Like Wilder himself, the Dreyfuss couple, *Stalag 17's* "Animal," and the janitor Kruhulik in *The Seven Year Itch* are American immigrants rather than European emigrants.

If Yiddish comes naturally to an American Jew of Wilder's generation, the Italian in *Avanti* is never more than a series of phrasebook snippets. This is fitting since Italy is here little more than a panacea for the stresses and strains of American corporatism, with a few Nixon jokes thrown in. It is significant that Wilder never provides subtitles when Rommel barks orders in *Five Graves to Cairo*. As in the POWs' play with German grammatical structures in *Stalag 17*—"Droppen sie dead"— Wilder always preserves a feel for the angular Prussian syllables as they strike the American ear.

Wilder's films also Americanize Europe by reducing its history to conflicts between individuals. What is compelling about the clash between communism and capitalism in *One, Two, Three* is the clash of personalities in which it is framed. Wilder is more than adept at charting the struggle to make Otto Piffl presentable to MacNamara's boss, yet the political events which motivate the episode remain hidden from view.

This "loss" of Europe, as it were, becomes glaring if we compare Wilder-ian psychical landscapes with the compelling use of Europe's voices and space in the work of a recent filmmaker like Kieslowski, a director who has worked from an equally sanctified sense of design.

Psychoanalytical jargon is talk which Wilder deploys fluently, if mockingly. To a large extent, films like *The Emperor Waltz*, *The Seven Year Itch* and *The Front Page* have contributed to a stock image of the "shrink" which has passed into popular mythology. Wilder's analysts embellish his preoccupation with the individual. Yet his mocking them could be read as the American's ironic view of a European modernist cul-ture from which Wilder himself emerged. However, he may mock the good doctor from Vienna, but films like *Double Indemnity* and *The Lost Weekend* offer psychological studies of great complexity.

It is significant that Wilder made films less frequently after 1965. By then, the postwar European art film had begun to make itself felt in American films and American minds. With Fellini, Bergman and Godard producing powerful examinations of European social relations, Wilder's "European" films increasingly came to resemble his oeuvre as an episode in the media's construction of the "global village," having pre-packaged real locations and sold them as part of the endless flow of electronic imagery through which we came to know the world in the second half of the century.

This replacement of the world by the word has a long pedigree. When Princess Swana picks up the phone in *Ninotchka* and asks for "Bal-zac 2769," we are reminded that Lubitsch's film is not a sociologically rigorous exploration of the headquarters of French civilization but, like Balzac's *Old Goriot*, an exploration of the myth of Paris, one of the most potent in the modern era. So potent is it that, fifteen years later, Wilder need only play *La Vie en Rose* through an open window in *Sabrina* to tell us where we are. By the end of his career, the inbreeding had spread to his own films. Shot on Corfu and financed from Germany, *Fedora* is "pre–New Wave, a face-lifted version of classical Hollywood cinema,"[7] and truly a reflection upon another Wilder film —*Sunset Blvd.*

It is not my purpose in this book to add to the excellent coverage of Wilder's "European" films undertaken by Sinyard and Turner and oth-ers, all of which can be found listed in the filmography. (I would, how-ever, urge whichever publisher has taken over BCW Publishing to reprint *Journey Down Sunset Boulevard*, and my readers to undertake strenuous efforts to obtain a copy.) Billy Wilder's films constitute a highly coher-ent and important body of work. I have chosen to return to a selection of that corpus in an attempt to shift critical emphasis away from the cocky little Viennese of legend to the hardworking Hollywood craftsman and rigorous commentator on the American scene in which role Billy Wilder is at his most absorbing and relevant. In this way I hope to evoke, through his best works, the chronicle he charts of American life in the middle years of the "American Century" which was born with him.

1

Hold Back the Dawn and *Ball of Fire*

Viewings of the films for which Billy Wilder co-wrote screenplays in the '30s reveal that many lay their action in Europe, or in the studio's idea of Europe. Wilder's 1941 screenplays for Mitchell Leisen's *Hold Back the Dawn* and Howard Hawks' *Ball of Fire* mark a turning point, since they offer progressively more realistic evocations of Wilder's adopted country.

One of Wilder's fondest memories is of the day in 1939 when he took the pledge of allegiance to the American system of government and became an American citizen. Such an honor had been hard won. In 1934, his six-month visitor's visa having expired, Wilder had to cross the Mexican border and kick his heels while the Department of Immigration and Naturalization pondered his papers.

This episode lends a certain piquancy to the opening scenes of *Hold Back the Dawn*. In it, Georges Iscovescu (Charles Boyer), a prospective immigrant, tells of a demoralizing wait for admission to America. With hindsight, Iscovescu's position seems symbolic of Wilder's at the time since, until 1941, he was seen by Paramount as a writer of witty and cosmopolitan comedies set in European hotels and casinos. But if Iscovescu awaited his moment, Wilder was beginning an examination of American society which has seldom been bettered in the history of the American cinema. And if *Hold Back the Dawn* lays Iscovescu's scheme to marry American school teacher Emmy Brown so as to become a U.S. citizen in the kind of ersatz reconstruction which typified foreign excursions in the

9

'30s, *Ball of Fire*'s fascination with American popular culture plants it firmly in U.S. soil.

But for all the seeming authenticity of Iscovescu's account, an oft-quoted anecdote bears repetition. There is a scene in the screenplay in which Iscovescu interrogates a cockroach in the manner of an immigration official as the roach walks up the wall of his hotel room. Wilder and collaborator Charles Brackett thought it a poignant encapsulation of the wretched circumstances of the transient, and of all prospective immigrants aching to begin a new life. However, reluctant for his ego to be compromised by a mere insect, star Boyer, in cahoots with Leisen, had the scene cut.

Ironically, such a fit of pique seems characteristic of the arrogant and self-serving Iscovescu. But the excision of this scene also reinforces the sense in which *Hold Back the Dawn*'s Mexico derives less of its power from a real country in which cockroaches do crawl around the hotel rooms of vain men than from the expedients of Paramount studio economics.

Let's look closely at that border town. In the opening scene we see a peon in a broad sombrero of the type commonly resorted to by Hollywood screenwriters to evoke the world south of the border. He is hunched before a U.S. border post which, significantly, resembles the gate at Paramount's main entrance. This identification becomes more significant if we view the film, as Bernard Dick does, as "pure Hollywood, where myth reverts to history, and history to myth, without violating each other's conventions or the laws of logic."[1] Typically, the street must be dusty. In keeping with the imperative that everything must be accountable to the screenplay's purposes, the "Hotel Esperanza," refuge to Iscovescu and a displaced community of European emigrants, evokes not only the "hope" of its Spanish name but, as Sinyard and Turner note, the artificial world language of Esperanto. This hotel of emigrants is reminiscent too of the cosmopolitan Paramount which had nurtured Wilder and which pointedly gives birth to *Hold Back the Dawn*.

The most interesting aspect of the film is that it is introduced through the history of its own genesis as a film. An unshaven Iscovescu arrives at Paramount Studios to pitch the story of his journey to Mitchell Leisen, who is at the time shooting *I Wanted Wings* while Veronica Lake and Brian Donlevy stand by on set.

Hold Back the Dawn then unfolds, following Iscovescu's narration. This is a novel device, foreshadowing the voice-overs in *Double Indemnity* and *Sunset Blvd.* and the studio locations in the latter film. Fortunately, although it draws attention to Leisen's film as a film, *Hold Back the Dawn* does step stealthily from reality into artifice in a relatively seamless fashion.

Blurring the border between film and reality will be a recurring theme throughout Wilder's oeuvre. So too are transformations of character. In *Hold Back the Dawn*, the reformation of Iscovescu following Emmy's near-fatal car crash tames the gigolo stereotype in which Boyer had been trading since the actor arrived in Hollywood. When Iscovescu changes from a sophisticated rake with a foreign accent to become a promisingly domesticated American male, he thus becomes qualified to enter the country. From the early '30s, Boyer had been seen by Americans as the amorous Continental, playing such a figure in *Mayerling* (1934), *The Garden of Allah* (1936), and most famously opposite Hedy Lamarr in *Algiers* (1938). His role in *Hold Back the Dawn* likely evoked such associations in the minds of American women emerging from the unromantic realities of the Depression. But the image of the wipers as they scrape the windscreen of Iscovescu and Emmy's honeymoon car, accompanied by his mantra "together, together, together" (later evoked to revive her in hospital), also carries the wider implication of an America and a Europe allied by their commitment to winning the war. Enraged by Boyer's refusal to play the cockroach scene, Wilder and Brackett cut down his role and played up Olivia de Havilland's as Emmy. As the plot reveals the extent of Iscovescu's exploitation of Emmy, this small-town innocent becomes the personification of the honeyed charms of American womanhood, announcing the blueprint for such as *The Lost Weekend*'s Helen St. James, *The Seven Year Itch*'s Helen Sherman and *Kiss Me, Stupid*'s Zelda Spooner. She also announced Wilder's imminent entry into the American hinterland.

Emmy could be the granddaughter of one of the kindly old academics in *Ball of Fire*, a relationship which would make her the symbolic country cousin of city slicker Sugarpuss O'Shea. As Sinyard and Turner point out, Emmy has an alter ego in Iscovescu's other partner, Anita (Paulette Goddard)—who like Sugarpuss, is a dancer. "Anita and Emmy seem almost two sides of the same coin, both dark, one sensual, the other inhibited, the one fire, the other water."[2] One is reminded of "ball of fire" Sugarpuss and lanky "glass of water" Bertram Potts.

What links Emmy to Sugarpuss is her unabashed Americanism. Lacking perhaps the color of Sugarpuss' New York locutions, Emmy's idiomatic "The children are as crossed as two sticks" carries the undeniable air of dog days beneath the shade tree. Entrenched in its artifice, beyond the studio prologue, *Hold Back the Dawn* offers little of America itself. Yet there is Emmy's talk of her home town of Azusa, California, a microcosm of America which learns and grows just as the wider society must. Not a million miles from Azusa, the title of Wilder and Thomas Monroe's story on which *Ball of Fire* is based was "*From A to Z.*"

Other clues which *Hold Back the Dawn* offers Iscovescu about the country north of the border are Emmy's monstrous charges. Approaching the cartoonish in their precociousness, one might charitably regard these children as the exuberant offspring of a society about to harness its energies in the service of a world role. There is also the immigration officer Hammock. Dogged in his pursuit of illegal aliens, this grubby civil servant has no imagination but all the meanness of the commonplace tyrant. In Hammock lies the blueprint for such Wilderian occupational cynics as Claims Manager Keyes in *Double Indemnity* and Private Investigator Purkey in *The Fortune Cookie*.

Another sign of the superiority of the land north of the border is Emmy's Chevrolet station wagon.[3] That it should break down beyond the aid of American mechanics and the reach of American spare parts seems to mirror Emmy's own helpless position. It is thus ironic that her alter ego Anita should at one point complain that "a woman wants a man, not a radiator cap." After all, both women have at different times fallen for the practically useless Iscovescu.

Aside from the emigrants' July 4 celebrations, and Professor Van den Luecken's rendition of Carl Sandburg's poem from the base of the Statue of Liberty, no more poignant an image of America exists in *Hold Back the Dawn* than Emmy's "clear and fresh" lake which "never gets stagnant when new streams are flowing in." For Iscovescu to qualify for entry he must learn to play a new role, stop lying and be himself, and it is Emmy's nature which sets him the example to do so. True to its watery theme, Emmy's love cleanses Iscovescu.

Notice how being in love and in America are equated with being honest. When Iscovescu and Emmy are on their honeymoon in Mexico, he is feigning affection for her, but when he crosses the border to be by her hospital bed, he crosses the line, as it were, between lying and truth-telling. Having expressed real concern for Emmy as a person, as opposed to a ticket north, their union becomes a genuine marriage as opposed to "immigration," Hammock no longer able to dispute Iscovescu's eligibility.

This dramatic distinction has an aesthetic dimension, mirroring the relationship between film and reality which *Hold Back the Dawn* explores. When Iscovescu sits on the border, he waits on what often resembles a film set, a contrivance, a lie. When he drives to Los Angeles following Emmy's accident, the film picks up credibility as well as pace. At one point, Iscovescu is even told that through the hospital window he can see downtown Hollywood itself.

The Americanized Wilder and the wordsmith Brackett clearly reveled in the investigation into the American linguistic undergrowth afforded by *Ball of Fire*. Hawks' film contains as fluent a celebration of American English as a Hollywood film has ever embarked upon. Yet slang is merely the most novel aspect of the film's intoxication with Americana. Aside from a drum solo by Gene Krupa, the film finds more than adequate cultural grist in the movies.

A comic melding of *Snow White and the Seven Dwarfs* and a routine gangster programmer, *Ball of Fire* was directed by a veteran of "American" subjects and shot away from Paramount at the Goldwyn Studios as part of a deal whereby Goldwyn got Wilder and Brackett in exchange for Paramount getting Gary Cooper for 1943's *For Whom the Bell Tolls*.

If Wilder's sure grasp of English shows in this piquant and fast-moving screenplay, he must have absorbed a lot about film pace and structure by observing Hawks at work: "I spent all the time on the set watching him shoot because I wanted to see a picture from beginning to end before I started directing myself."[4] However, although the dynamics involved in placing a woman in amongst an all-male group are very Hawksian, Sugarpuss' scheme and the relationship she has with Bertram are very Wilderian.

Ball of Fire also displays the talent for engrossing the viewer that we find in classic Wilder films such as *Double Indemnity* and *Sunset Blvd.* There is a vitality here that is missing from the sluggish *Hold Back the Dawn*. There is too a richer sense of place than in the Leisen film. If the characters' talk is peppered with references to Central Park, the Washington Bridge and the Holland Tunnel, the action finds English professor Bertram Potts seeking examples of slang on recognizable American street corners, in bars and nightclubs, and on the New York subway at rush hour.

Like *Hold Back the Dawn*, *Ball of Fire* also embroiders upon film history. True to the "screwball" tradition in which Hawks had excelled in the '30s, the camerawork is conventional, the lighting high and bright, and a woman meets and falls for a gauche and engrossed boffin before thoroughly disrupting his life. Also resembling a spoof gangster movie out of Warner Bros. in the late '30s, *Ball of Fire* vacillates between generically required scenes of Sugarpuss O'Shea's "daddy" Joe Lilac on the run or being grilled by the police, and wacky scenes of the professors back at the Foundation. Indeed, in contrast with the manner in which Lilac and his hoods push Sugarpuss around, these gracious old men recall the glutinous charm of the Disney dwarves as well as the three old innocents of *Ninotchka*, who also encourage the young lovers. When Lilac's men Duke Pastrami and "Asthma" Anderson (crime movie regulars Dan Duryea and Ralph Peters), burst in and instruct the professors to line up facing the wall, Professor Magenbruch (cuddly S. Z. Sakall) remembers the St. Valentine's Day Massacre, an event which has been consecrated by the movies, not least by Wilder himself.

In order to blend into her adopted refuge, Sugarpuss (Barbara Stanwyck) tells Bertram to see her as "just another apple." Earlier in 1941, Stanwyck made the screwball comedy *The Lady Eve* in which her confidence trickster heroine led the ophiologist hero "Hopsy" Pike to the brink of social and financial ruin. The allusion to an apple could be read as a reference to the book of Genesis from which screenwriter-director Preston Sturges also derived his title. Clearly, "Pottsy" Potts recalls Stanwyck's last victim "Hopsy" Pike. Also in 1941, Stanwyck made *Meet John Doe* in which her cunning journalist exploits another innocent, played by Gary Cooper. *Ball of Fire* adds to and refines Stanwyck's essays on smart women beguiling dumb men, but as Wilder would later demonstrate, her potential was itself becoming ripe for subversion.

Ball of Fire continues the exploration of innocence versus experience begun in *Hold Back the Dawn*. From the Wilderian "meet-cute" in which Bertram, immersed in his research, knocks on Sugarpuss' dressing room door in search of her colorful locutions while Lilac's hoods conceal themselves, he becomes the brainy sucker to her worldly moll. No brasher a sense of the gracelessness of modern life can be found in *Ball of Fire* than the moment when she takes her coat off in the Foundation's drab library, knocking him backwards with the skimpiest and most garish evening gown ever seen.

If Emmy grows a little worldlier through knowing Iscovescu, Bertram (another educator) also grows up a little after meeting and falling in love with Sugarpuss. When the police turn up at the New Jersey trailer park in search of Lilac's moll, Bertram, despite feeling betrayed by Sugarpuss, puts them off her trail much as Emmy magnanimously declines to betray Iscovescu to the immigration officials when Anita reveals his duplicity.

While Sugarpuss represents the racy modern world, Bertram, with

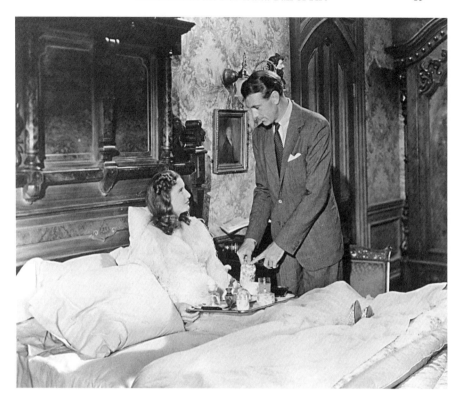

A nation subverted. Sugarpuss O'Shea (Barbara Stanwyck) twists Bertram Potts (Gary Cooper) around her little finger in *Ball of Fire*, United Artists, 1941.

his starched shirts and old-fashioned fisticuffs, represents turn-of-the-century gentility. "I walked in the Park till the sun came up over the East '60s," he tells her in the preamble to his giving her an engagement ring (such a contrast to that which Iscovescu passes from Anita to Emmy). Compare Bertram's words with the newspaper headline — "Professor bridegroom carries ball of fire across state line" — and the collision between old and new becomes clearer. "If our work goes slowly, it is because the world goes too fast," Bertram tells Miss Totten, daughter of the Foundation's founder. His confession to Sugarpuss, and the words from Shakespeare's Richard III which he has engraved on the ring, betray a literary sensibility which is most comfortable when words are written down, hence his preoccupation with collecting slang. It is important to Bertram that he "light out" into the wider world to keep his article on slang alive (in contrast with his heart which has become deadened by years of bookish dust). And the screenplay is at pains to approve of such honesty. Notice how much more lively is Sugarpuss and the garbage man's jive talk than the ponderous answers the professors offer for the garbage man's "Korn Krunchies Quizzola." "On account of because" may outrage grammatical law, but its Brooklyn ring is unmistakable. In *Ball of Fire*, Wilder's early immersion in American sports, radio and popular music receives its first real airing. Its celebration of slang is infectious: featuring phrases such as "Screaming Mimis" (jitters); "Patch my pantywaist" (term of amazement); and "What's buzzin', cousin?" and whole conjugations like "Scram, scraw, skedaddle." Even Carl Sandburg is recalled for a quote — "Slang is a language that takes off its coat, spits on its hands, and gets to work"— which would not look out of place in H. L. Mencken's seminal *The American Language*.

The idealized language which Bertram uses to describe his feelings is one strand of *Ball of Fire's* preoccupation with romantic love. The garbage man describes his girlfriend as the "mouse, the dish, the smooch." Later, during a seminar led by Bertram, the professor is offered examples of corny language between the sexes. And during Bertram's bachelor party, Professor Oddly (Richard Haydn) reminisces about his marriage to Genevieve, followed by the old men's rendition of the once-popular song. Each of these scenes is written as a lesson for the unworldly Bertram. At the same time as he learns something new about the possibilities of the American language, he gains insight in a sentimental education. That love and language are so closely bound offers a powerful hint about Wilder's feelings for America, as well as his working philosophy.

In Wilder's first film as director — *The Major and the Minor*— a little girl at Grand Central Station asks her mother to buy her a movie magazine with a cover story entitled "Why Charles Boyer Hates Women." It is an obvious dig at the actor who maligned Wilder's screenplay, but also at directors who were not sufficiently attentive to the screenplay. The rise of Billy Wilder in 1942 would be a resounding blow for the writers.

2

The Major and the Minor

If there is any truth in the observation that a decade's cultural and intellectual style does not become apparent until around the second or third year, the mood of *The Major and the Minor* now looks poised somewhere between the sexual intrigues of the Depression comedy and the heroic sentiments of the wartime recruiting poster.

Wilder likes to relate that, on the night before he was due to begin shooting, he suffered so badly from nerves that he went to Ernst Lubitsch in desperation. The following day a delegation of fellow European directors visited Wilder at Lubitsch's behest to offer encouragement, but held up shooting for hours. But if this blessing had been conferred by the man whose sly Continental innuendo had been Wilder's model in the '30s, *The Major and the Minor*'s cosmopolitan charms are as motivated by plain and simple American pragmatism as Lindbergh's flight to Paris.

As Wilder describes it, "They said, 'Let Wilder make a picture and then he'll go back to writing.' Everyone expected me to make something 'Fancy-schmancy.' Yet I made something commercial. I brought back the most saleable hunk of celluloid I could."[1] Shot in the narrative-driven, key-lit vein which was to become Wilder's no-nonsense style as his career progressed, *The Major and the Minor* trades in familiar ruses and deceptions.

Compare the prologue of *Ninotchka*: "This picture takes place in Paris in those wonderful days when a siren was a brunette and not an alarm ... and if a Frenchman turned out the light it was not on account of an air raid,"[2] with that of *The Major and the Minor*: "The Dutch bought New York from the Indians in 1626 and by May 1941 there

17

wasn't an Indian left who regretted it." Notice how the saucy delicacy of the first has given way to the conspicuous gripe of the second. If Brackett and Wilder's script for Lubitsch celebrates the happy promiscuity of Catholic Paris, their script for *The Major and the Minor* carries all the suspicion in Protestant middle-America for such "fast" ethics.

It is tempting to conclude that, at the core of *The Major and the Minor* is the American heartland, yet this is not the case. What lies at the heart of this warm and witty film is merely the comforting idea of small-town America. As with Wilder's "Paris" and "Berlin" in such "European" projects as *Love in the Afternoon* and *One, Two, Three*, Wilder fails to get sufficiently near to "Stevenson, Iowa" to let us hear it and breathe it in. Such an impression is foretold by the deadbeat whom Susan/Sue-Sue Applegate (Ginger Rogers) enlists to buy her ticket for "Stevenson, Idaho." Sue-Sue may as well live anywhere west of the Mississippi. Although we see Mrs Applegate's folksy Midwestern porch, with its hammock and a sign advertising home-made preserves, we never experience Susan's relief as she pulls into Stevenson after all the trouble she has experienced getting there. Whatever truth exists on that porch consists more in the sincere rapport between actress Rogers and her actual mother Lela (Mrs. Applegate) than in a mood which, after all, would have been culturally alien to an Austrian Jew. Wilder eventually destroys the illusion of comfort by having Susan's intended, Will Duffy, throw a rock at the light bulb illuminating the porch. When we next find ourselves at such a porch in a Wilder movie, it is peopled by Zelda's parents, the gargoyles Mr. and Mrs. Pettibone in *Kiss Me, Stupid*. Too urbane for the Fordian moment toward which the Applegate porch drifts, Wilder's Americana works easier within a more cosmopolitan frame of reference. His "Stevenson" serves as a mere metaphor for the myriad "burgs," with their picket fences and feed and grain stores which litter the American heartland and from which the bulk of Wilder's audience hails. In the Wilderian universe, "Stevenson" could be the twin of Emmy Brown's Azusa and is just as nominal. Yet Wilder and Brackett's denigration of the sexual and financial chicanery of New York played well in the boondocks, filling "countless theaters with the lovely and important sound of laughter."[3]

More substantial is *The Major and the Minor*'s celebration of the purposeful like. Arguably, *Hold Back the Dawn*, *Ball of Fire* and *The Major and the Minor* feature Wilder's progressive departure from the sophisticated European idlers of the Paramount '30s, and an ever closer involvement with American innocents in their search for themselves.

Professionally adrift in New York, Susan Applegate has had 25 jobs in a year but still cannot realize her potential. Finally, she decides to return to her hometown. But finding that the rail fare exceeds the amount she had saved for the purpose, Susan disguises herself as an 11-year-old and travels on a half-fare. Returning from his base from Washington after failing to secure an active posting, Major Phillip Kirby (Ray Milland) inadvertently befriends the vulnerable "Sue-Sue." Like such Wilderian characters as Don Birnam in *The Lost Weekend, Some Like It Hot's* Sugar Kane and Bud and Fran in *The Apartment,* Susan and Phillip are stranded somewhere between where they started and whom they wish to be.

As Sinyard and Turner have acknowledged, the scene in which Susan is solicited in a plush hotel room in New York by her egg shampoo client, Mr. Osborne, carries more than a whiff of the urban loneliness and moral disintegration which Wilder explores more fully in films like *Double Indemnity* and *The Apartment.* Such a metropolitan malaise is a mood with which Wilder is at home, and it frequently afflicts characters who lack controlling interest in their own lives.

In the opening shot of *The Major and the Minor,* we see a street sign reading "E.47/Park Ave." As the camera descends to street level, we find Susan making her way to her appointment with Osborne. The seedy air of a prostitute going to rendezvous with a trick is hard to escape. Yet the absence of a constructive sense of purpose seems to be universal. The deadbeat takes advantage of her. The lonely Osborne, his wife away at what he sees as pointless air raid drill practice, tries to seduce her with witless innuendo. The ticket-collectors on the train pester Sue-Sue with a zeal which foresees Wilderian inquisitors like the insurance claims manager in *Double Indemnity,* and the private detective in *The Fortune Cookie.* Cadet Osborne and his comrades at Wallace Military Institute pursue Sue-Sue partly because racked with pubescent desire, and partly to alleviate the tedium of endless military ABC exercises. Their lack of purpose recalls the anarchy caused by Emmy's bored charges in *Hold Back the Dawn,* while Colonel Hill and the tutors under him at Wallace Military recall the redundant elders at the Foundation in *Ball of Fire.*

A sense of purpose in Wilder is perennially achieved through the imperatives of a personal scheme. The charm of *The Major and the Minor* results largely from the prankish nature of Sue-Sue's scheme, as compared with murkier Wilder scenarios. Susan is initially intent only upon returning to Stevenson. But at the Institute, Lucy Hill, sister to Phillip's fiancée Pamela, encourages Susan to help her dislodge Phillip from a partner who wants him to remain a tutor and out of active service. By achieving this, Susan will free Phillip's sense of purpose, free another man for the looming war effort and, eventually, secure him romantically for herself.

The purposelessness which bedevils Iscovescu and Bertram in *Hold Back the Dawn* and *Ball of Fire* could be regarded, given their year of release, as a veiled call to arms for an America still undecided about her role in the European war. *The Major and the Minor* completed shooting a month before the Japanese attack on Pearl Harbor, making its commitment to Phillip's military future an obvious appeal to Americans to get involved. Susan and Lucy's scheme also marks the film as deeply patriotic in another sense; individual endeavor is an ingrained American ideal. And if these two think things through for themselves, their chief antagonist could be regarded as displaying the same undemocratic principles in her controlling influence over Phillip as did the Japanese in China and the Germans in Poland. Notice how she imposes her own construction on events when Phillip attempts to explain on the train why he has an 11-year-old in his compartment. Later, with two progressively more intricate high angle shots, Wilder shows Pamela watching Susan return from a dance where she has agreed to a tryst with Phillip. Again, such shots have the effect of imposing a point of view which is entirely in keeping with Pamela's undemocratic nature.

One of the most entertaining scenes in Ginger Rogers' career is that in which Sue-Sue lures the cadet on switchboard duty away so as to put a call through to Washington, as Pamela, in order to secure Phillip's transfer to an active posting. Wilder's insistence upon casting this lithe and strong-willed actress in the role demonstrates what a shrewd eye the director had for playing with, and often subverting, the resonance which the star system afforded. Sue-Sue lures the cadet into securing a radio so that they can jive together, clicking her feet on the makeshift dance floor with a bobbysoxer dexterity completely consonant with the pop sensibility of the era. Demonstrating too his great ear for the appropriate tune for the occasion, Wilder opts for "A Woman's a Two-Face," underlining Sue-Sue's not inconsiderable feat of impersonating first the cadet and then Pamela as she pulls off her coup. It is not often that a comic scene such as this is wrought in such a way as to draw out this much suspense. Indeed, at the moment when Sue-Sue is discovered out by a horde of annoyed callers whose calls she has misdirected, the scene begins to evoke, significantly, the feats of bravado of many a future war film.

Sue-Sue saves Phillip from a marriage in which his independence is likely to be severely curtailed. Although his fate beyond the altar is not spelled out, there are enough clues. When we first see the patrician Pamela, she is driving a 1941 Chevrolet Special DeLuxe like the school bus driven by Emmy in *Hold Back the Dawn*. In the passenger seat sits her father, the head of the Institute. Sitting in the driver's seat, in the vehicle as in life, characterizes Pamela as a manipulator whose position enables her to direct the grown-up children who run the Institute. Indeed, the irony of Wilder and Brackett's deft title revolves around the reversal of roles implied by Pamela's, and temporarily Susan's, control over the Major.

"Those three days she spent with us, it seemed as if ... spring had enrolled at Wallace Military; everything came alive from the youngest

A nation beguiled. Sue-Sue Applegate (Ginger Rogers, second from the right) twists Wallace Military Institute around her little finger in *The Major and the Minor*, Paramount Pictures, 1942. *Center to right:* Pamela Hill (Rita Johnson, center) remains skeptical; between the ladies Major Phillip Kirby (Ray Milland) remains charmed; Colonel Hill (Edward Fielding, right) remains calm.

cadet to the oldest cannon." Phillip's words are a concentrated statement of the film's melange of wistful yearning and sexual innuendo. But
as well as being a touching tribute to Susan, they are a tribute to the
myopic "Uncle" Phillip's innocence. Defective in one eye, but determined to see action even if his first battle loses him his fiancee, his independence of outlook finds expression in his response to Sue-Sue. While
practically all the men and boys she meets want only to seduce her, and
Lucy and Pamela see her disguise for the fakery it is, only Phillip is blind
to the situation, treating her with undiscriminating tenderness. Like
C. C. Baxter in *The Apartment* and Harry Hinkle in *The Fortune Cookie*,
Phillip is at heart a dopey romantic, making Milland something of a
prototype for the Jack Lemmon persona which Wilder was to mold in
the '60s. Falling asleep by counting dwarves, a ploy meant to put Sue-
Sue to sleep, is typical. As is falling for his maternal dancing teacher at
the age of 12. As Sinyard and Turner point out, Wilder's mockery of the
American military tradition, as expressed in the overall failure of the
officer class to penetrate Susan's disguise, can be read as a caution to an
America grown complacent in a hostile world.

Rogers' performance teeters between girlhood and womanhood.
Her achievement as Sue-Sue resides in her ability to make series of
almost invisible transitions from charming little girl to charming young
woman. This achievement takes place not only through the inevitable
change of clothes, but often with merely a look. When Phillip lectures
Sue-Sue on the power that light bulbs wield over moths and young girls
wield over young boys, Sue-Sue stands a little too close to him, the juve-
nile boredom on her face imperceptibly altering to a knowing smile.
Comparisons between *The Major and the Minor*'s study of pedophilic
attraction and Nabokov's in *Lolita* have been frequent and, as Sinyard
and Turner have notes, Phillip's marriage proposal so as to be near Sue-
Sue forges the strongest link between the texts.[4] However, the vital
difference between Nabokov's novel and Wilder's film is that Phillip's
innocence will not allow him to admit that he is sexually attracted to Sue-
Sue, because his circumstances will not admit to his being a man, with
all the responsibility this brings. Lacking the means to act purposefully
in his straitened relationship with Pamela has had a blunting effect upon
his perception of his role. In some subterranean way he loves Susan/Sue-
Sue, but he has allowed his adult perceptions to be commandeered by
Pamela's controlling influence over what he says and does. Still immersed
in the deceptions which the two-faced Pamela has wrought, he tells Sue-
Sue: "It's not often that a boy my age gets a smile from someone whizzing

by in a kiddy car." Such a remark carries a whiff of American naiveté which is missing from the cadets' talk of the Maginot Line and the fall of Sedan as they attempt to seduce Sue-Sue. Leaving aside the veiled plea for a fallen France which their line of attack undoubtedly evokes, it is clearly too bookish for the pragmatic Sue-Sue and too Lubitschian for the age of anxiety which was looming. In contrast, the scene in which Susan, her heart aflutter, rushes downstairs for her nocturnal assignation with the Major contains a forlorn romanticism which is quintessentially Wilderian.

There is something a little unreal about Wallace Military Institute. While the parade ground seems too redolent of a middle-European "gymnasium" for the Midwest, the ballroom, with its waltzing officers and finishing school girls with Veronica Lake "peek-a-boo" hairdos, feels like a slice of subverted Lubitschiana. If Wilder mocks the elitism which stands between the genteel Major Phillip Kirby and a working girl like Susan Applegate, the film's vernacular sensibility attests to Wilder's love of democratic modern American idioms. Another character, Wilbur, is a little boy at Grand Central Station who, when told by his mother to tell the man in the ticket booth how old he is, refuses, telling the man that he is a "Corn Pickles Secret Operator" and doesn't have to tell anyone how old he is. In the uncontrollable Wilbur, innocence has bred a healthy independence. In *Double Indemnity* Wilder will examine the cost of independence.

3

Double Indemnity

Double Indemnity is one of Wilder's finest films and is widely acknowledged to be one of the greatest films ever made. In it, Wilder's preoccupation with the underside of American enterprise is most fully articulated. As supple as a well-crafted sentence, the film has all the elegance and efficiency of the best mainstream Hollywood product. In *Double Indemnity* there is thorough harmony between plot, theme, space and time, and each word and gesture has its place.

In the novella by James M. Cain which formed the basis for Wilder and Raymond Chandler's screenplay, morbid, grasping Phyllis Nirdlinger lures her lover, insurance salesman Walter Huff, into selling her husband a "double indemnity" accident policy before they both murder him and elope with the proceeds. The screenplay is said to have been influenced by the Snyder-Gray murder case of the '20s, and it is easy to imagine its appeal for a young Wilder immersed in the coarser narratives from the American undergrowth.

So coarse was it that the patrician Charles Brackett, Wilder's collaborator since 1938, refused to work on the project. Casting around for a suitable partner in Brackett's, as well as Cain's, absence led the film's Associate Producer Joseph Sistrom to a novelist whose work oozed the southern Californian social climate. Chandler, a tweedy and reclusive English-educated writer of the "tough" school of pre-war American crime fiction, was signed to co-write *Double Indemnity*'s screenplay in 1943. The collaboration between the energetic and efficient Wilder and the alcoholic Chandler was fraught. Suffice to say that Chandler hated Hollywood, did not understand screenwriting technique, was unused to

To the end of the line... Walter Neff (Fred MacMurray) and Phyllis Dietrichson (Barbara Stanwyck) in *Double Indemnity*, Paramount Pictures, 1944.

the regime at Paramount's "Writers' Building," and didn't like Billy Wilder, yet the Chandler and Wilder views of the story meshed.

Chandler's fiction is a breed of fatalistic realism. His characters inhabit a world in which morality is almost entirely relative. But if their laconic conversation was considered "modern" when it appeared in the pulp fiction of the '30s, Chandler's detectives bore the honorable stamp of medieval knights. Chandler could also write dialogue which rings out as it is read, being spoken by real American urban types who eat, breathe, love and die.

The dialogue in *Double Indemnity* is some of the richest in any Wilder film. It does not waste a word in setting scenes and fashioning them to the motion of the plot. Indeed, the screenplay's power consists in a punchy melange of Chandler's deft descriptions, Cain's rootless Californian ethos, and the vigor of Wilderian storytelling.

When bored housewife Phyllis Dietrichson (Stanwyck) and confident young insurance salesman Walter Neff (MacMurray) meet, they discuss her husband's risky work as an oil executive. Their talk of falling crown blocks and snapping casing lines owes much of it authenticity to Chandler's 13-year stint with an oil company. Later, in the office of President Norton at Walter's employer "Pacific All-Risk," Claims Manager Keyes (Robinson) offers a breathtaking exposition of the workings of an actuarial table which was probably informed by Chandler's experience as an accountant. As must have the officialese in Walter's later dictaphone confession to Keyes. When Phyllis offers Walter iced tea, he asks whether she is English. This would also suggest the hand of Chandler, an anglophile whose work betrays an obsession with the genteel habits of the mythical English rose. Walter's voice-over as he leaves: "How could I have known that murder can sometimes smell like honeysuckle,"[1] contains a forlorn romanticism which suffuses both Chandler's fiction and Wilder's films.

If Cain's novella seems overwrought and tends to read better than it would play, the screenplay blends coherence and irony in a concise and pungent way. Written in the vein of stylized realism, as Richard Schickel put it: "Their dialogue is just a little jazzier than we are likely to hear in life."[2] And in Bernard Dick's words: "Neff talks ... in units of thought, where the ideas generate their own rhythm and their own grammar,"[3] resulting in a heady mixture of raciness and realism. Neff talks in images tautly cut to fit an atmosphere of dread. "We have a guy in our office named Keyes. For him a set-up like that would be just like a slice of rare roast beef. In three minutes he'd know it wasn't an accident. In ten minutes you'd be sitting under the hot lights. In half-an-hour you'd be signing your name to a confession."[4] When Walter and Phyllis banter in her lounge, they use a traffic violation as a metaphor for his pursuit of her, creating a lively "American" subtext which translates longing into a combative exchange in a universal clash of wills. Indeed, *Double Indemnity* is the most cutting examination Wilder ever offered of a society bent upon verbal and economic one-upmanship, Walter and Phyllis' exchanges capturing the "mechanical, hard-edged quality of mating rituals in America."[5]

However, the world of *Double Indemnity* is a mixed economy, and its characters are also implicated in a network of chance and circumstance over which they have little control. When Walter's jaunty Dodge coupe — so like him in character — runs the stoplight on a downtown intersection, we are compelled into a one-way journey into paranoia and despair. "Straight down the line" is an incantation which Walter and Phyllis utter throughout the film. The "machinery"[6] of their conspiracy motivates conversations riddled with references to implacable mechanisms. And in a met-narrational sense, the machinery could just as easily refer to the seamless plotting of Wilder's film.

Few Hollywood films of the classical period are as compelling as *Double Indemnity*. If the novel flashback structure of the screenplay creates the impression of a fixed set of fortunes which can only go one way, Wilder's editing helped. His technique was to "cut in the camera," or shoot only so much film as was necessary for the scene, a tendency facilitated by his close rapport with Doane Harrison, his editor during the last two films. As Steve Seidman writes: "Action is usually played out in medium shot and relatively long takes.... The editing here is not to provide symbolic effect but to break master scenes into a variety of set-ups. This "invisible editing" maintains a narrative flow and also anticipates the viewer's conception of the action taking place on the screen. Dissolves are used to establish even the shortest passages of time."[7] Before Walter leaves his apartment to meet Phyllis and murder Dietrichson, there is a series of dissolves in which he places cards in the doorbell and phone exchange box which will drop if they ring. He then leaves using the service stairs, having made a point of asking the garage attendant to clean his car. If asked, Charlie will say that Walter was working in his apartment all night. Such attention to detail has seldom been reflected in so thoroughgoing a fashion as in Wilder's own methods. At the close of the film, there was to have been a scene in which Walter goes to the gas chamber. Typically, Wilder set it up taking the minutest care to authenticate the execution.

Such realism, considered shocking when the film was previewed, represents one of the most pungent aesthetic currents in Wilder's '40s films, inviting the viewer to look into, as well as at, these masterpieces of narrative cinema. The extent of *Double Indemnity*'s sense of tragic inevitability seems to occur in the final scene when Walter, dying from a gunshot wound inflicted by Phyllis, asks Keyes whether he is to be nursed back to health so that he can walk into the gas chamber on his own two feet. His assumption that Dietrichson and Phyllis' deaths will result in his own is not merely the outcome of stringent plotting, but would seem to make redundant the moral distinction between illegal murder and judicial execution. The dread of the prospect of death by cyanide capsule which is reiterated throughout, and the look of horror in Phyllis' eyes when she realizes that she is going to be shot to death are analogous fears. Doubtless, the intended thrust of the film's moral logic is Old Testament — murder must be paid for by death — but strict adherence to Old Testament law is likely to be rare among contemporary Wilder audiences. And with the pall of death — a legacy of the Cain source — hanging over the film generally, *Double Indemnity* could perhaps be seen as one of the most searing indictments of capital punishment prior to Tim Robbins' *Dead Man Walking*.

Other than that necessary to advance the plot, the film offers little information about its characters' pasts. But when Lola Dietrichson, Phyllis' stepdaughter, reveals to Walter that Phyllis caused the death of the first Mrs Dietrichson some time before, it hints at much about Phyllis.

If Walter was "trying to think with your brains, Keyes,"[8] Phyllis must co-opt Walter's expertise in order to attempt release from a buried existence. The critical line on Phyllis Dietrichson has traditionally claimed that she is an alluring and treacherous woman who cynically uses Walter as an escape route from her marital responsibilities, and in order to earn a fast $100,000.

Seen through Walter's eyes, Phyllis is a woman of moments and parts: her perfume, her gold anklet, her silky blonde hair, her fawning appeal to his professionalism. For many critics, she is an upmarket slut. But perhaps, like the "Minor" Susan Applegate, Phyllis simply lacks direction, having at some point been corrupted in her search for a purpose in life. It is significant that we only ever understand Phyllis in terms of Walter's voice-over, or Keyes' account of her actions. In the light of the progressive examinations of neurotic women offered by Woody Allen in recent years. It is perhaps time to re-examine the character and a Wilder ending which has been the subject of critical debate for over 40 years.

Dolores Paley in Allen's *Crimes and Misdemeanors* recalls the libidinous woman of film noir of whom Phyllis is the archetype. Like Phyllis, Dolores has a shady past, and in both films revelations about their pasts trigger these characters' downfalls, each death emerging as a result of scrupulously refined schemes. Like Dolores, Phyllis is truly a tragic figure. If loneliness and insecurity hasten Dolores' death, Phyllis' need for security has driven her into marriage to a drunk twice her age — "I wanted a home. Why not?"[9]

In keeping with both films' tight structures, both characters are defined by the unscrupulous liaisons which compel them. If Phyllis married someone with the temperament of a ringside failure, she has an affair with someone who will eventually murder her. Phyllis lacks the language of self-discovery which feminism has offered characters of Dolores' generation. Consequently, she is unable to determine her own future and so must have a man to steer her, a situation resulting in his rejection of her when her crude self-assertion becomes problematic.

Rather than acting to avert a predestined future, Phyllis can only react to a hellish past and present. Having swapped uncertainty for a comfortable home and a two-car garage, she finds herself married to a workaholic who drinks in bed and beats her up.[10]

"Phyllis is the stone-hearted whore goddess who appears in many Wilder films.... She has killed once before, kills again and is prepared to do so at any time; she is the user who discards whatever is used up and looks for something else to use...."[11] She is a "destructively lurid female."[12] Male critics tend to harp on the fact that Phyllis is guilty of using her sexuality to ensnare Walter. But, reared in a pre-feminist culture in which women were the appendages of men, their virtues defined by men, Phyllis lacks the know-how to be anything more than an accessory in Walter's imagination. The inability to start her car without his help illustrates the extent of her helplessness. Since Phyllis' story comes to us via Walter's voice-over, we are made to go along with his judgment of her. In Keyes' opinion, she murdered Dietrichson with Nino Zachetti, Lola's boyfriend, and what's good enough for Keyes is good enough for Walter. Phyllis must function in a world in which the paternalistic Keyes, the husband Dietrichson, and the lovers Walter and Nino, take moral precedence over the woman Phyllis, even whilst this patriarchal order is being challenged by the prodigal Walter. In the warlike universe of the film, Walter challenges the husband and his surrogate father Keyes with the object of installing another man — himself — in their place.

As a woman, Phyllis is not only untrustworthy, according to the misogynist Keyes, but unable to act without copious instructions from Walter. His handing her a drink with the words, "See if you can carry this as far as the living room,"[13] and her "I never know what's in the ice-box"[14] state her redundancy and alienation, even in her own home. Given the critical emphasis on Phyllis' manipulation of Walter, it seems ironic that it is she who complains that his scheme to kill Dietrichson, claim the insurance and be together is actually tearing them apart. As emotionally confused as she may be, Phyllis is more aware of her feelings than the hard-boiled Walter, as her demonstrations of affection suggest. In their final scene, it seems more likely that Phyllis lacks the maturity to know the difference between love and like than that she is feigning affection. Her admission: "No, I never loved you, Walter. Not you, or anybody else"[15] is not so much a confession to insecurity as to stunted emotional development. "I used you, just as you said"[16] again borrows his words as a sign of her helplessness. She embraces him for the last time, and she is emotionally as much as physically hurt when he puts the gun against her and fires, this scene being one of the most romantically forlorn in all Wilder for its grotesque parody of meaningful verbal and sexual intercourse. Phyllis' confession of love is sad because it contrasts so poignantly with such exchanges as when he asks the name of her perfume. "I don't know. I bought it in Ensenada," she replies, unable even to find a scent which is her own and could be theirs. A fundamental part of their romantic currency thus remains a mere purchase in a cheap border town.

Walter rejects her confession in favor of Keyes' suspicion. His "Save it. I'm telling this"[17] obliquely calls to mind his voice-over, but also embodies the masculine attempt to control feminine wiles. The overriding tragedy of Phyllis' existence is that she may only have discovered herself at the point at which she is about to die. Giving Walter the gun with which he shoots her effectively enables him to "execute" her for her crimes against the patriarchal order. Even if we read Phyllis as insincere and unchanged by events, she is still tragic for having failed to realize just how buried her existence has been. If not, her confession is her first and final moment of truth.

Transformations of character often occur in Wilder, but this final scene between Phyllis and Walter is one of his most equivocal closures. We are left with the possibility of Phyllis' redemption without needing the obligatory happy ending which, for some, has marred other Wilder films. As far as the patriarchal order is concerned, it is enough that

Walter finds redemption by confessing, while Lola is left to settle down with Nino and assume the conventional feminine role. What Phyllis' death suggests, as a character in *Crimes and Misdemeanors* reflects, is that wisdom comes to some suddenly.

Phyllis has been read as a cautionary cinematic reflection of the self-sufficient American woman of the war years. Newly independent and with money to spare, such an individual could enjoy her freedom without fear of social censure. The implications for fidelity to absent husbands and lovers are clear. The patriarchal order which Phyllis disrupts supports a system of property relations which defines a woman as the property of a man's estate. Phyllis' acquiescence in the system's logic — Money = Fulfillment — makes her the docile vector of attitudes which neither she nor any of her sex have instituted. Far from relieving her plight, Walter has simply added to her perennial despair. In stressing her allure so as to ensnare a breadwinner, the artfully named Phyllis Dietrichson[18] has blindly complied with the rules of a game which she did not invent but must play in order simply to exist.

Weltered in the phony claims which pile up on his desk, Barton Keyes is steeped in a conviction that humans are infinitely deceitful. "You wouldn't even say today's Tuesday without you looked at the calendar ... and then you would find out what company printed the calendar, then find out if their calendar checks with the world almanac's calendar,"[19] Walter teases. Keyes was almost married once, but the "little man" inside who tells him when a claim is crooked led him to have his fiancee investigated.

Aside from his ravenous enthusiasm for the job, the only feeling which Keyes allows himself is his fondness for Walter, the son he never had. Beneath the sordid heterosexual drama of *Double Indemnity*, a touching father-son dynamic is tersely expressed through the ritual in which Walter lights the cigars of the matchless Keyes. Poignantly reversed in the final scene, the dying Walter takes out a blood-stained cigarette and Keyes lights it. "You know why you didn't figure this one, Keyes?.... The guy you were looking for was too close. He was right across the desk from you." "Closer than that, Walter," Keyes corrects him.[20] In a film in which one couple's rapport feels more like warfare than love, this scene recalls those battlefield clinches in which dying buddies can be hugged by their comrades.[21] Indeed, Parker Tyler argues for Keyes as symbolic of the Allied "claim adjuster"[22] who was to preside over Germany's war guilt in 1945. If his matches always seem to ignite in Keyes' pocket, the claims manager's ferreting talent has blown up in his face. As much a victim of the plot's mechanical logic as Walter, the hard-headed ratio-nalist finds that his rationalism leads straight back to the one chink in his rational armor.[23] In a film in which all the characters are trapped and none can avoid being hurt, the "machinery" denies the individual the will to evade being crushed. Keyes is therefore bound to lose the "son" whom he has cultivated and who now lies dying by the hand of a woman. As Andrew Sarris writes, "for all its deadpan stoicism *Double Indemnity* strikes uncommonly sweet chords of male camaraderie in its final con-frontation."[24] Keyes wants Walter to steer clear of women, and at one point offers him a martini with two olives in a Freudian allusion which, for once in a Wilder film, doesn't mock psychoanalysis.

Double Indemnity is a grim screenplay, but there is humor, partic-ularly in the first half of the film. Keyes' scene with Norton deftly announces the real brains behind "Pacific All-Risk" reinforcing the film's portrait of a deeply competitive society, and revealing Wilder's slangy touch. Following Norton's tactless exchange with the morning Phyllis, Keyes ridicules him: "Nice going, Mr. Norton. You sure carried that ball. Only you fumbled on the goal line. Then you heaved an illegal forward pass and got thrown for a 40-yard loss. Now you can't pick yourself up because you haven't got a leg to stand on."[25] Much of the dialogue stems from this ease with mid-century American vernacular. As Schickel noted, Wilder "heard something wild and strange ... what sounded like clichés to the native-born sounded like fresh metaphors to a wry spirit listen-ing closely."[26]

The reviewer in the *Monthly Film Bulletin* of August 1944 may have been responsible for the first reference to a thriller style which would flower in the immediate post-war period, then pass into film-critical legend, and continue to be reworked in some degree in every crime film since. Their observation — "some sensitive use of camera and light-ing"[27] — may seem tentative today, but it remains a portent of the effect which this influential film would have on postwar critics and audiences.

By 1944, Hollywood monochrome photography had reached the zenith in sound cinema which it reached in silent cinema around 1926. *Double Indemnity* cinematographer John Seitz had himself been a cam-eraman since the silent period. His work here is some of the most efficient ever achieved in the classical period. Notice the economy with which Walter's abrupt departure from Phyllis and her hold over him is con-tained in a shot over her shoulder as she watches him leave. As Sinyard and Turner have detected, the film's dichotomy between an active and open masculine world, the world of Keyes and Neff, and a sensuous and enclosed feminine world, is graphically pointed up in a medium shot down the corridor in which Phyllis waits concealed to the left of the frame behind Walter's open apartment door, while Keyes stands to the right of the frame in the freedom of the corridor. But however conventional the shooting style ultimately is, *Double Indemnity* is not without some striking effects. While the "plunging" shot onto acres of desks in the ground floor well at "Pacific All-Risk" looks forward to the ever grosser angles of '50s film noir, the bars of light slicing through cigar smoke and the aluminum "dust" which Seitz used to catch the sunlight in the Dietrichson lounge, remain key moments in the evolution of a genre. Another beautiful effect is that of the streetlights flickering on Phyllis' blonde hair as she stares impassively out of the gloom on what, with hindsight, we might regard as the night on which film noir was born.

Always attentive to the mise-en-scène, Wilder provided a rich clutter of light fixtures, "in" trays, dictaphones, water coolers, desk lamps and prints of prize fighters to adorn the sets at "Pacific All-Risk" and Walter's apartment. In keeping with the actor placement in the corridor shot, we see Phyllis clandestinely call Walter while, to her right, supermarket customers mill. There is a cut to Keyes' office in which he stands to Walter's right while Walter bluffs his way through an incoming call. While maintaining the visual pattern from scene to scene, the sense that law-abiding citizens are "in the right" is subtly reinforced.

An especially significant aspect of the mise-en-scène is Wilder's use of real locations, unusual in 1944 and a tendency which anticipates the realism of such directors as Elia Kazan and Sidney Lumet in the post-war period. This can be most poignantly felt at "Jerry's Market" on Melrose Avenue near Paramount Studios. The reproduced supermarket interior, with its range of goods — amounting to around a million ration points — powerfully underlines the theme of greed which *Double Indemnity* explores. And in this claustrophobic film there is a real sense of release as Phyllis enters "Jerry's Market," cars and pedestrians moving along Melrose Avenue behind her. But most memorable are such scenes as the dumping of Dietrichson's body at the railroad tracks, shot "night-for-night" for maximum gloom. Or Walter's nocturnal drive through careering traffic. It is at such moments that *Double Indemnity* reaches back toward the poetic realism of Zola or the Renoir of *La Bête Humaine*.

Paramount gave Wilder carte blanche to cast *Double Indemnity*, and again he knew the value of stretching the actor to fit the roles he had in mind. When "heavy" specialist George Raft and Paramount regular Alan Ladd declined to play Walter, Wilder began a process of badgering second-tier musical comedy lead Fred MacMurray. As Maurice Zolotow tells it, "He wanted a nice, sweet, wisecracking guy who had larceny and lust inside his Rotarian go-getter skin. A guy with a grin. He went after MacMurray ... in the commissary, in his dressing room, at home.... He wore MacMurray down. MacMurray said yes, knowing that the executive head of Paramount West Coast production, Y. Frank Freeman, wouldn't let him. Mr. Freeman hated immoral movies. He considered this a dirty movie."[28]

What Wilder had in mind when casting Barbara Stanwyck as Phyllis Dietrichson were films like *Ball of Fire* and *The Lady Eve* in which she had essayed, albeit comically, smart women who beguile innocent men. Dressed in a shrill blonde wig and delivering lines that always hit the spot, Phyllis seemed a natural, if dangerous, progression from these roles.

Edward G. Robinson is spellbinding as Barton Keyes. His staccato delivery echoes the belligerent gangster roles of the '30s almost as though the character had resolutely swapped allegiance in later life. The self-satisfied shadow of Keyes in waistcoat and reading-glasses roving along the corridors of "Pacific All-Risk" contains all the dynamism of the Little Caesar, but replaces his ruthless violence with ruthless logic. Robinson does not simply parody himself here, however, but he actually earns his keep in the role; talking to policy-holders, answering the phone, and sifting through statistics and claims for compensation.

Double Indemnity was released in America in September 1944, its bleak vision perhaps a truer reflection of the long and bloody war in which, in 1941, the boyish Major Kirby was keen to get involved, than many films of its year. With its scenario of redemption through violence, the film now seems more aligned with the times than such as *Meet Me in St. Louis* and *Going My Way*, a comedy with Bong Crosby and Barry Fitzgerald as feuding parish priests. For Parker Tyler, *Double Indemnity* seems the expression of a latent public perception that war, whatever the motive, is murder, and murder represents a psychological kink. (Hence the wartime perception of Hitler as "crazy" or barmy, depending upon which side of the Atlantic you were on.) Without doubt, the film brought moral and physical carnage onto American screens as an aggressive couple engaged in a sexual analogy of real warfare. It is not tenderness but murderous frustration when Walter seizes and kisses Phyllis. Never before had apparently decent suburbanites been portrayed as killers.

In this film all are on the make. Tyler writes of Walter: "Neff's pathological illusion is one of the diseases of American culture: that salesmanship can be aesthetic value."[29] Phyllis' last words are: "I'm not asking you to buy. Just hold me close,"[30] for once attempting to escape even the trading of one's words in favor of a status quo based upon love and personal value. *Double Indemnity*'s suburbia could be seen as the prototype of the social consensus whose values Richard Nixon and Ronald Reagan represented in the '70s and '80s, one endorsing the Watergate cover-up and the other the culture of insider trading. Arguably, Walter engages in a little insider trading in a Wilderian universe in which the best-laid plan is often a lonely fist shaking at God.

4

The Lost Weekend

This 1945 film marked a turning point for Wilder. Winning four Oscars — Best Picture, Best Director, Best Actor and Best Screenplay — *The Lost Weekend* brought him well and truly into the front line of Hollywood directing talent. But watching this study of an alcoholic's life-cycle today we are struck by its resemblance to such issue-based Hollywood fare as *Kramer vs. Kramer* (1979) and *When a Man Loves a Woman* (1994). Tackling an "important" theme, boasting a bout of histrionics from star Ray Milland as Birnam, and appealing to a mass audience, Wilder made a film with "Oscar winner" written all over it.

Based upon Charles Jackson's Dostoyevskian novel, *The Lost Weekend* follows a drunken writer through a four-day drinking spree. Abandoned by brother Wick (Phillip Terry) who leaves on the country cure designed for Don, and abandoning faithful girlfriend Helen (Jane Wyman), Don gravitates from bar to bar before ending up in "Hangover Plaza," the alcoholic ward of Bellevue Hospital. Finally, as he contemplates shooting himself, Helen persuades him once more to give the writer in him another chance.

Leaving aside the over-emphatic production values — the Miklós Rózsa score, state-of-the-art realism, happy ending — *The Lost Weekend* remains a compelling portrait of a man's decline and eventual resurrection. The film may have been tailored to a mass audience, but the lifestyle and aspirations which it charts are unique. If the characters in *Double Indemnity* mislead one another by what they say, Don Birnam misleads himself. The circular visual scheme identified by Sinyard and Turner reflects a very writerly malaise. Don's "vicious circles" (the concentric rings his glass leaves on a bar; the balls outside a pawnbrokers'; the spherical light bulbs he grabs as he falls downstairs; a close-up of his eye; the cyclical shape of the film) are the result of a grave lack of confidence. And so he drinks to achieve creative satisfaction, a habit which makes him physically ill, grounding him once more in his low self-esteem. He drinks to preserve the creative fiction. A self-deceiving take upon typically duplicitous Wilderian characters, the film finds drink making Don a writer by proxy.

A key scene has Helen confronted with Don's drinking for the first time. In the scene Don comes out of a cupboard in which he has been hiding while Wick covers for him. It is key because it reveals the drinker and the writer to be two sides of the same personality. It is a step forward because it primes us for the final scene in which Helen persuades Don-the-writer not to pull the trigger on Don-the-drunk, thereby killing the person he always wanted to be. If Walter Neff becomes "whole" by confessing, Don must stop talking his fiction out in bars and write it out. When the potential suicide writes his suicide note to Wick, it is a refreshing, ordered contrast with his meandering barroom talk. This "writing out" of the death wish is an act (as opposed to mere talk) which becomes the prelude to his resurrection back at the apartment, the film having come full circle. It is a moment of self-awareness which surely signals the healing of the fracture.

Duplicity prevents Wilderian characters from seeing their true potential. Walter could have a great career but for his scheme to defraud the company. C. C. Baxter in *The Apartment* believes that the route to self-advancement lies in debasing himself. Baxter and Birnam, like Major Kirby, are children in the bodies of men, men who have not yet learned to be self-governing. In an allusion to Milland's last role in a Wilder project, Don tells liquor store proprietor Mr. Brophy that he is not a minor and demands service. It is a pathetic gesture from an adult whose younger brother keeps him. Don's delusion is doubly pathetic because it has blinded him to the obvious course of action: to seek self-awareness on the written page.

Basil Wright perceptively sees in Wilder's notoriously ambiguous ending a reflection of America's predicament at the end of World War II. Winning the war brought on all the anxiety attached to playing a fuller role than ever amidst the "realpolitik" of a troubled postwar world. *The Lost Weekend* was released barely weeks after peace was declared. Among the film's audiences would have been ex-servicemen dizzied by the sudden loss of comradeship and uncomplicated purpose which the war had offered. It becomes possible, perhaps, to read Don's drinking as a metaphor for the fraught transition through which returning service-men had to pass in order to settle down and build a future. In failing to establish himself, Don stands outside America's burgeoning post-war prosperity. In this light, it becomes easy to feel his horror at having to confront Helen's conformist Ohio parents.

The Lost Weekend is a rare example of a Hollywood film which acknowledges class divisions in American society. Less about alcoholism as a physically wasting disease, its focus dwells relentlessly upon Don's social decline. The film is littered with exchanges illustrating the differing conditions and aspirations of its protagonists. A number of critics have rightly commented upon the color which Wilder and Brackett's screen-play affords peripheral characters like Nat, Gloria and Bim. This is a ten-dency wholly in keeping with the camera's odyssey through the proletarian streets and tenements of its New York setting. According to

The end of the line. Don Birnam (Ray Milland), the middle-class aesthete seeks inspiration in postwar realism. Nat the barman (Howard da Silva) tells him a thing or two about *nostalgie de la boue* in *The Lost Weekend*.

barman Nat (Howard da Silva), Don treats his "high class" *Time* researcher girlfriend like dirt. Yet he nevertheless finds "Mr. Birnam" a compelling bar companion, listening agog to the pitiful and pretentious clutter of an addled but educated mind. Lacking an education but secure in his calling, the churchgoing Nat has the democratic kindness which we find in such Wilderian working people as Mr. and Mrs. Dreyfuss in *The Apartment* and Polly the Pistol in *Kiss Me, Stupid.* Like Helen and Gloria, Nat is torn between disgust for the drunk and pity for the writer and the man. Returning Don's lost typewriter, therefore, becomes wholly motivated by Nat's nature, while his innuendo when finding Helen at the apartment is wholly in keeping with the banter of his barroom background.

Gloria's ignorance of *Hamlet* is compensated for, as far as she knows, by knowing 44th Street where the play is running. Doris Dowling's studied performance as the jive-talking loser is, along with Nat, one of *The Lost Weekend*'s joys. Her clipped vernacular is a perfect foil for Don's bloated prose, while her mixture of style and vulnerability is a refreshing antidote to Helen's unequivocal stiff upper lip. Her "Thanks — but no thanks" is reputed to have become a gimmick in America for a season. The ease of this proletarian environment finds expression in Don's wish to take Nat and "all that goes with you" to Wick's pastoral retreat.

By comparison, the Bellevue nurse Bim (Frank Faylen) is one of the more cutting portraits of a gay character in Hollywood history. Sardonically hinting at Don's likely fate on the ward, and revelling in dipsomania's clinical details, Bim becomes a soft-spoken symbol of Don's loss of "manhood." It is significant that, in the film's opening scene, Don describes his and Wick's relationship as "the nurse and the invalid." To heterosexual '40s audiences, homosexuality may have smacked of an urban nether world of non-conformists and dropouts, the flipside to a "normal" heterosexual bourgeois lifestyle. In a film essaying the stages of a corrupted manhood, it would have been tempting to read the fussy but ineffectual Wick and the sinister and effeminate Bim as compass points on a descent into hell. On Don's road to ruin, neighbors whisper, and when he is caught attempting to steal someone's purse, he becomes riffraff to be thrown into the street. At Bellevue ("a halfway prison, halfway hospital"), Don is undressed alongside a black patient, another reminder of his social decline. When he tells Nat that "I'm on that merry-go-round and have to ride it all the way," we are reminded of Walter and Phyllis' trolley car ride. The gas chamber may not be at the end of Don's ride, but anonymity and disgrace dog his every step.

Rome — Open City, a 1945 film, heralded the impact of Italian neo-realism, with its location shooting, realist camerawork, exploration of social problems, plots conveying the rhythms of everyday life, and convincing use of non-professional actors. While pursuing Hollywood's own explorations of real space such as in *Double Indemnity*, *The Lost Weekend* further demonstrates Wilder's commercial acumen by subsuming innovation into mainstream filmmaking and giving it wider currency.

Fluent with the efficient mise-en-scène which characterizes all of Wilder's best films, the circular visual scheme betrays Wilder's scrupulous hand even 3000 miles from Hollywood on the streets of Manhattan. Aside from the balls which beckon from every pawnbroker on Don's odyssey down Third Avenue to pawn his typewriter, the clock he passes reinforces the prospect of a life lived out of step. Marked by authentic street signs, Don's sweaty, unshaven progress from 55th to 110th charts the same growing sense of despair we find in Walter's confession. Shot with a concealed camera using available light and the fastest film stock, Don begins to resemble the emasculated father searching for his lost bicycle in the neo-realist classic *The Bicycle Thieves*. Duplicating the interior of a genuine Manhattan watering hole at Paramount added to the realism. But if some shots in *The Lost Weekend* — Don seen through a rack of bottles in a liquor store, a doomladen close-up of his whisky glass — seem self-consciously artistic for a Wilder film, we might see them now as the over-emphatic miscalculations of a film with a showy, laurel-seeking agenda.

The most powerful sequence in the film is that in which Don is incarcerated in Bellevue, escapes, and suffers withdrawal symptoms back at the apartment. Here, its synthesis of melodrama and realism tips over into a hybrid pitched somewhere between a horror film and film noir. "Delirium is a disease of the night," Bim tells Don. Delirium, whether fuelled by fear, jealousy, or a gunshot wound, will become the common fate of many a hapless drifter in films noirs of the '40s and '50s, and in Bellevue exist the conditions which give rise to it. Notice the grille shadow which "imprisons" Don as torch lights stab the air when the nurses brutally restrain a screaming patient. Notice how the dawn exterior of the hospital foresees the dark street of 1950's *The Asphalt Jungle*, the gargantuan arches and wrought ironwork of this nineteenth century city hinting at Gothic nightmare. The staircase leading to Gloria's apartment, with the streetlight pouring in through the doorway, looks back to the expressionist sets of '20s German films, and forward to the dimly-lit corridors and staircases of high film noir. Finally, Don's hallucination in which a wheeling bat devours a mouse places *The Lost Weekend* in a direct line of descent from the Gothicism of the '30s Universal horror cycle. Mining the rich vein of modernist angst from which Jackson's novel sprang, and re-reading it through John Seitz's play of light and darkness, *The Lost Weekend* becomes a key moment in Wilder's rebellion against the polite and seemly in American cinema.

But whilst the mood and look of Don's decline betray aspects of Hollywood's maturing style, there remains a tension in the film between the decadent and the consensual. Less effective is an often pleasant but often intrusive score which mars, especially, Don's walk down Third Avenue and his hallucination. More economic use of the theremin-drenched music might have allowed the dust and detritus of Wilder's street scene to tell its own story. As Sinyard and Turner have observed, the generic stereotype to which "nice girl" Helen conforms allows no room for more interesting development of her character. Indeed, we wonder what motivates this smart and pretty young woman to fall in love with a drunk with, apparently, precious little career promise. Consonant with the film's mainstream appeal, Helen signals conformity to the simplistic convention that, with Wick out of the way, Don will be saved by the faith and love of a good woman, just as Iscovescu was saved from himself by Emmy. The Wilderian "meet-cute" in which Don and Helen get their coats mixed up at the opera, and as the crowds disperse stand waiting for each other in the lobby, packs a poignant punch. But Helen remains on the edge of the drama, her lifebelt — "There is no cure apart from just stopping" — sounding ominously like Nancy Reagan's glib "Just Say No" campaign against drug abuse. What we detect in Wyman's performance are the seeds of forthcoming turns in such middle-class melodramas as *Magnificent Obsession* and *All That Heaven Allows*.

Ray Milland's performance subverts the portrait of boyish irresponsibility coaxed out of him in *The Major and the Minor*, and provides a link with such compromised heroes as out-of-work writer Joe Gillis in *Sunset Blvd.* and man-child C. C. Baxter in *The Apartment*. In 1964 on the release of *Kiss Me, Stupid*, Joan Didion wrote: "The Wilder world is one seen at dawn through a hangover, a world of cheap double entendres and stale smoke, and drinks in which the ice has melted: the true country of despair."[1] As flawed as this uneven film is, *The Lost Weekend* remains central to Wilder's chronicle of postwar urban American fortunes.

5

Sunset Blvd.

Sunset Blvd. begins as unemployed screenwriter Joe Gillis (William Holden) is fished out of a Sunset Blvd. swimming pool by the police. In a voice-over narration, Joe tells in flashback how he was driven to ghost the "return" screenplay of a mad silent film star, Norma Desmond (Gloria Swanson), sacrificing the love of fellow screenwriter Betty Schaefer (Nancy Olson) and his career. It seems appropriate that the dead narrator's last assignment should have been ghosting someone else's work. Indeed, as his arrival when Norma expects the undertaker for her dead chimp suggests, Joe henceforth becomes an emasculated alter ego, a man and a hero by proxy. His status as a narrator who is dead is never problematic because we are used to disembodied narration in classical cinema, and the supernatural edge which the device lends the film is consonant with the grotesque half-lives led by Norma and her manservant Max von Mayerling (Erich von Stroheim).

Joe Gillis is one of Wilder's most flawed heroes, a character whose easy veneer of corruption entrances us to follow its grubby course to his downfall. Like Don Birnam, his misfortune lies in wanting to be successful in a difficult profession. Like Walter Neff's, his scheme is doomed because it draws him into the orbit of a character more wayward than he. What was compelling about these characters in Wilder's time was that they challenged conventional notions of screen heroism. *Sunset Blvd.* startled audiences in 1950 with its realistic portraits of Tinseltown and a protagonist antihero forced into a no-man's land somewhere between honor and depravity. Joe is cynical, but as we see when he attempts to hawk his story around the studios and begs contacts for a loan to rescue

The latest assignment. Joe Gillis (William Holden) contemplates a long-term contract (no options) while Norma Desmond (Gloria Swanson) outlines the conditions in *Sunset Blvd.*

his precious car from the finance company, few in this town are willing to offer credit to a "failure" without adequate credits. Arguably, like the many poses adopted by the famous and not-so-famous in Hollywood, Joe's sardonic narration is a pose, an effect like the voice-over itself. "Poor dope. He'd always wanted a pool. Well, in the end he got himself a pool, only the price turned out to be a little high." This detachment is a way of dealing with his failure to make the grade. But being an insider, he knows the formulaic excesses to which the denizens of Hollywood are prone and has become immured in the role-playing. His cynicism is a kind of attitudinal strategy, a literary riposte to the prevailing phoniness. The idealism he once had lies hidden beneath the pose. Notice how he bluffs about his and Betty's screenplay before affirming that it is good and "will play." His affection for Betty re-awakens the need to write original dialogue. Part of the tragedy of the film is that such compassion comes too little and too late to save either of them.

Hollywood is and always has been a community in which the rewards are high and the competition fierce. Some writers on *Sunset Blvd.* have taken the view that Norma represents a tightly-knit Old Hollywood in which the tenor was gentler and the atmosphere more tolerant of the creative sensibility. Joe and Betty's New Hollywood, by comparison, is harsher and peopled with slick mediocrities. But given the rewards involved, and given the pressures American society traditionally places on the individual to succeed, how much gentler could Hollywood have been in the '20s when stars were earning $18,000 a week and the community seethed with young hopefuls? Reminiscing about his own rise in the '30s, Wilder complained to Charles Higham that "Today we spend 80 per cent of the time making deals and 20 per cent making pictures."[1] Wilder's nostalgia for his own early career is understandable, as Norma's is for her own. But given the establishment of corporate structures in Hollywood from around 1914, it rapidly became an industry in which the logistics of business took precedence. As Janet Staiger explains, "This new system centralized the control of production under the management of a producer, a work position distinct from staff directors. The producer used a very detailed shooting script, the continuity script, to plan and budget the entire film shot-by-shot before any major set construction, crew selection, or shooting started. This system, while part of a major shift in US business practices to 'scientific management,' was also due to … the techniques for achieving continuity, verisimilitude, and narrative dominance and clarity (coalescing) to create what we call the classical Hollywood film."[2] But, despite the corporate atmosphere, there is too a gentler tenor at work in the New Hollywood. When Joe flees the musty imprisonment of 10086 Sunset Blvd. to be with Artie Green and Betty on New Year's Eve, the warm and relaxed atmosphere brings tremendous release. The soundtrack crowded with naturalistic overlapping dialogue, and the frame choked with "below the line" technicians and struggling writers and starlets, Wilder emphatically contrasts Artie's boozy goodwill with the precious and claustrophobic rituals of Norma's mansion. New Hollywood may seem mean in certain circles, but of all his acquaintances, Artie is the only one prepared to lend Joe money, while Betty goes so far as to fall in love with him.

Sinyard and Turner argue that, by comparison with Norma, Betty is dull and conventional. But if they each arose out of rich though differing traditions, both Norma and Betty are nevertheless steeped in the imagination which exposure to the movies has wrought. Whilst Norma is a product of the fabulous tradition of '20s exotica, with its emphasis on the sumptuous image of the unattainable star, Betty is a product of the snappy and socially aware dialogue tradition (Wilder's own), and the realism of the post-war message movie — "I just think a picture should say a little something." As co-screenwriter Charles Brackett wrote when defending the film against its detractors, "The exact purpose of (Betty) ... was to embody the ideals of the town, the passion for truth on the screen, the passion for good pictures."[3] It is significant that two key plot developments are signaled by written messages. Betty receives a telegram from Artie proposing marriage, prompting her to own up to Joe that she loves him. And Norma realizes that Joe has been going every night to work on the screenplay with Betty when she discovers it in his room. Whilst the screenplay makes no definitive statement to the effect that the movies have improved since Norma's heyday, it is clear from Joe and Betty's redemptive collaboration (as opposed to Joe's cynical collaboration on Norma's "silly hodgepodge of melodramatic plots") what Wilder feels about the evolution of the American cinema. As *Sunset Blvd.* shows, and its Oscars for Best Original Story and Screenplay recognize, pictures require the discipline of strong writing to make them accessible to an audience.

Wilder may not here have been interested in making serious statements about the evolution of the cinema, but *Sunset Blvd.* is "about" Hollywood on a level other than that of mere narration. As Dick writes, Wilder always used aspects of his stars in the characters they have played. He found something weak in Fred MacMurray and Ray Milland which was perfect for the roles of Walter Neff and Don Birnam. Barbara Stanwyck traced a trajectory from compromise to corruption thanks to Wilder's rewriting of her screen image. Holden's languishing career until *Sunset Blvd.* finds poignant echoes in Joe's. In Norma Desmond, Wilder created the "diva incarnate"[4] who, like Swanson, never regained the star privilege once the talkies came in. In a scene culminating in perhaps the film's definitive shot, Norma and Joe watch Swanson herself in *Queen Kelly*, her and Stroheim's 1928 masterpiece. As Sinyard and Turner put it, "What is being watched on that private screen, by Joe and by us, is both a Max von Mayerling and an Erich von Stroheim creation."[5] Hence, the rapture which Joe observes on Kitty Kelly's face on the flickering screen becomes echoed in Norma's as she rises, standing in the projector beam to rail at the producers, "the masterminds" who have "forgotten what a star looks like," Joe's cigarette smoke rising as though from the genie's lamp in a slice of silent exotica. Norma's megalomania has rendered her unable to distinguish between life and film and so she acts compulsively. At one point she reenacts her role as a '20s bathing beauty, her spinning parasol giddily filling the frame like her dream fills the film. Norma Desmond is a concentrated statement of the film's wholesale melding of the real with the reel, and here is *Sunset Blvd.*'s most compelling performance: Swanson revelling in Norma's color but never descending into the ridiculous. Scorning dialogue — "I can say anything I want with my eyes" — she has said everything with her face and body before she even speaks.

Ironically for Norma but deeply fortuitous for us, however, Swanson gets the film's most famous line. Drawing herself up haughtily, Norma/Gloria's eyes widen before looking down her nose at the unemployed writer — "I *am* big. It's the pictures that got small." Having grown up in the midst of the extravagant silent acting tradition, Norma's postures are not simply allusions to another age but a piece of that age in this age. As Bosley Crowther wrote, "Norma Desmond ... has been in archaeological seclusion for a couple of decades when the story begins, [representing] more than the delusions of one old star. She represents the ostentation and arrogance of a whole generation of film-makers which has passed — a generation who produced a glittering output of gaudy trumperies and vast vulgarities, yet whose craftsmen assumed the postures and played the roles of great creators of Art."[6] Seen in this historical light, the contrasting performances of Desmond/Swanson and Holden and Olson plot a map of the first 50 years of Hollywood screen acting. Swanson reinforces the tragedy of Norma by playing her in early scenes as a dotty but likable maternal aunt, ironically distancing her from us — "those wonderful people out there in the dark" — the more demented she becomes. Notice how she strikes the appropriate pose in the mirror (a familiar distancing device in movies), before confronting the departing Joe for their final big scene, her flourishes seeming redundant as he pragmatically packs his bags and returns her presents. Finally, when Norma descends the stairs to meet the press, thinking they are the crew filming her return to the screen, the actress has become utterly severed from her audience and the world around her. When she reaches the cameras, she addresses DeMille who is not even present. In few other scenes in post-war cinema does one filmic generation stare with such stupefaction at its predecessors, and in few films prior to the '60s are we made so aware that what we are watching is a roll of celluloid.

Bridging the generations is Max, played by Stroheim, an actor who, since his decline as a director in the late '20s, turned in memorable performances, including that as Rommel in Wilder's *Five Graves to Cairo*.

Playing Max von Mayerling in the stiff Prussian manner in which his '20s publicity image was cast, Stroheim is, once again, the teuton of movie legend. Yet the precision hides an undercurrent of humiliation. In the '20s, Max informs Joe, there were three great directors — "D. W. Griffith, DeMille and Max von Mayerling." Once married to Norma, his discovery, when she left him Max became her manservant, and the unendurable pathos of his position can be felt in every stifled gesture. The name "von Mayerling" was, undoubtedly, inspired by the Austrian von Stroheim's claim that he had been one of the military guard sent to investigate the reputed suicide of Crown Prince Rudolf at Mayerling in the late nineteenth century. This incorporation of historical repute into film fiction adds a further layer to *Sunset Blvd.*'s resonance. Notice too how Wilder reinforces Stroheim's image with profile close-ups. Long an admirer of Stroheim's own portraits of a Hapsburg grandeur rotting from beneath, Wilder privileges Max with the task of guarding the Hollywood heritage which Norma represents against the ravages of contemporary reality. It is he who writes her fan letters. It is he who demands entrance to the Paramount lot when she takes DeMille her screenplay. It is he who "directs" the press cameramen as she descends the staircase for her final scene. It is he who controls reality's access to fantasy by monitoring Betty's frantic phone calls to Joe.

The control exerted by Max over events could be seen as a reflection of the control exerted by Wilder over *Sunset Blvd.* It is significant that he chose Buster Keaton for the scene in which Norma plays bridge with the other silent figures H. B. Warner, Hedda Hopper and Anna Q. Nilsson, not simply because he is another great name from the era, but because he was a great bridge player. Such a casting decision was made less out of disrespect than out of Wilder's habitual sense of precision. *Sunset Blvd.* is not so much littered with allusions for allusion's sake. Rather, it is infused with the drama and realism which such allusions reinforce. For Wilder, ever aware of changing trends, the scene in which DeMille counsels Norma about the changes which filmmaking has undergone makes sense because DeMille had been a father figure to Swanson in her young days, and was a familiar figure on Paramount sound stages in 1950. The lesson implicit in this scene, ignored by Norma but learned by Wilder, is that one must meet and even exceed those changes if one is to survive in the business. Thus, in a film which straddles film history and film practice, this cluttered and busy scene becomes a commentary both about Norma's predicament and contemporary Hollywood.

Elsewhere, Joe mentions Paramount players Alan Ladd and William Demarest, while Wilder has the trysting Joe and Betty stroll through Paramount's exterior set of Washington Square. In 1949 William Wyler made Henry James' novel *Washington Square* into *The Heiress*, starring Olivia de Havilland and Montgomery Clift. Prior to entering the set, Joe and Betty almost kiss, Joe coyly telling her to stay at least two feet away if they are to complete the screenplay. In *The Heiress* the heroine memorably shuns her suitor, subjecting herself to a life of loneliness. This allusion gains further poignancy when we remember that Clift was Wilder's original choice for the role of Joe. Knowing that Joe's rejection of Betty will perpetuate his isolation only adds to the poignancy. Again, the common ground between film drama and film history is knowingly exploited by Wilder.

Sunset Blvd. also relates thematically to the Wilder and Brackett-scripted *Hold Back the Dawn*. Both films are set in varying degrees in contemporary Hollywood, and both deal in usury and self-deception. Norma and Emmy both fall for gigolos who use them, if in Norma's case the usury is to some extent two-way. Norma and Emmy also represent American cultural archetypes, the movie star and the schoolteacher. The schoolteachers with "their threadbare lives, their struggles" in Joe and Betty's screenplay remind us of Emmy and idealistic teachers in Hollywood movies ranging from turn-of-the-century Americana to Ford westerns. The deployment of such archetypes is a measure of Wilder's ability to contribute to the cultural genealogy of the movies, as evidenced by his making *Sunset Blvd.*, a film echoed in 1992 by Robert Altman's *The Player*.

Nancy Olson turned 22 during the summer when *Sunset Blvd.* appeared. This is also Betty's age, adding to the film's importation of reality onto film. It is unfortunate that her and Joe's screenplay never materializes because the teacher whom she outlines begins to show promise as an original character. Often playing "sensible sorts and waiting wives,"[7] the pragmatism which Olson brings to Betty becomes the more appealing the more Norma goes into fantastic decline. For post-war generations, it has been the Bettys, Arties and Joes who have helped fashion the classic (and not-so-classic though cherished) American movies of the era. In the foreword to *Script Girls*, Lizzie Francke's book about Hollywood's women screenwriters, Francke pays tribute to the ambitious and hard-working Betty, a woman whose common sense long ago accustomed her to her failure as an actor but promise as a scenarist. For Joe and for us, Betty's enthusiasm is infectious. At Artie's New Year's Eve party she and Joe contrive a hammy scene from a pre-war melodrama with a tongue-in-cheek aplomb which, nevertheless, transmits Betty's love of the pitfalls and possibilities of the medium. And, as a studio story reader, she is well aware of the pitfalls. "It's from hunger," she informs producer Sheldrake of Joe's story pitch. "You take Plot 27A. Make it glossy, make it slick." She damns it, but not without knowing what constitutes good writing for the screen, as she later discovers in his forgotten story which she and Joe will adapt. During their tryst, Joe describes her as smelling like "freshly-laundered linen handkerchiefs or a brand new automobile." Rejecting conventional romantic dialogue, Betty inspires Joe with the poetry of the American modernist tradition which has inspired Wilder.

It is tempting to wonder why the intelligent Betty does not ask Joe what he is doing when he is not with her, given his newfound affluence and sudden departures. It is a question which the screenplay forestalls to some extent by casting Betty as a schematic portrait of innocence. Notice that when Joe tries to explain his situation she doesn't want to

"This is good. I think it will play." Joe Gillis polishes that scene while Betty Schaefer (Nancy Olson) fixes that coffee in *Sunset Blvd.*

know. Her innocence has become delusional. Arguably, both she and Norma are victims of the same neurosis. They are mired in Hollywood fictions and so cannot escape from their roles. The difference between them is a matter of style, but it also resides in Betty's dynamism. She knows how to move with the times (as has Wilder); Norma is stuck in a rut, albeit a rut of glittering dimensions. Joe matters to Betty, but, as she tells him at Schwab's, she is not working on their screenplay simply for his sake, but because there may be something in it for her. It may take time, but Betty will get over Joe's death by immersing herself more fully in her career in the movies, in illusions but not delusions. What we find in Betty is a link between the wisecracking career girl of the '30s social comedy and the empowered professional woman of the '50s. If Norma's "childish scrawl" is pathetic to the eye, Betty is writing dialogue that will play. In Betty is borne out Wilder's conviction that, in the '30s, "the pictorial art was facilitated by the dialogue."[8]

In *Sunset Blvd.* Wilder does not try to plumb the psychological depths of the characters. The overall impression is of a storyteller telling the story in as slick and economical a way as he knows how. Like *Double Indemnity*, the film begins sensationally and flashes back to the history of the crime, reading like a tabloid murder in which appearances are torn loose to expose the rot beneath. In Joe's scathing words about the newspaper men who arrive to gloat over his bullet-ridden corpse there is a touch of the ire with which he damns the studios who refuse to hire him, plus a hint towards *Ace in the Hole*, the indictment of "yellow" journalism Wilder was rehearsing at the time. *Sunset Blvd.* begins with a pan across the name stenciled on the sidewalk as on a grubby packing crate, and the film proceeds to a host of real Hollywood locations: the screenwriters' hangout, Schwab's Pharmacy; Norma's mansion (reputedly once J. Paul Getty's); a sound stage and the Spanish Gate at Paramount Studios; and a section of the Bel Air Golf Course. "Sunset Blvd., Los Angeles, California" Joe affirms as police cars career towards us in an opening scene recalling *Double Indemnity*. Like *Double Indemnity*, *Sunset Blvd.* is replete with the garish sunlight of southern California. Norma's dusty abode reminds us of the Dietrichson house and, before that, the musty Foundation which entombs Bertram in *Ball of Fire*.

Predictably, there are no effects sought for effect's sake. Yet, in its quiet way, *Sunset Blvd.* is technically very accomplished. The famous shot of Joe's body lying as though on a sheet of glass seen, apparently, from the bottom of Norma's pool contains a macabre hint at Joe's inability to break into the Hollywood mainstream as well as hinting at the film's superficial allure. Using a mirror suspended on the floor of the pool and mounting the camera alongside to film the reflection created a visual flourish which is properly motivated and suggests a director still young enough to be excited by the medium. For Norma and Joe's New Year's Eve tango sequence, cameraman John Seitz used a dance dolly, enabling Swanson and Holden to take a 360 degree turn around the room. Appropriately, Seitz introduced the idea when filming Valentino dancing the tango in *The Four Horsemen of the Apocalypse* in 1921. This link is echoed in Norma's talk of Valentino during the sequence.

Elsewhere, Seitz achieved exceptional depth of field by "latensification,"[9] a process in which an undeveloped image on underexposed stock is exposed to low-grade light until a denser image results. Depth of field is frequently used to reiterate Norma and Max's domination of Joe, as in the shot in which Max appears in the doorway at Schwab's to beckon him back to Norma. Like mummified artifacts, Norma's bandaged wrists appear in the foreground as Joe paces ineffectually in the background, both in sharp focus. Earlier, Max's white-gloved hands calmly play the organ in the foreground, Joe dashing across the garden to the strains of Bach's *Toccata* to demand to know why his belongings have been moved into Norma's house without his say-so. In contrast with the tactile informality of Artie's apartment, the formal architecture of Norma's mansion is continually reiterated in depth of field compositions. Latensification also enabled night exteriors to be shot at night rather than by day with filters. Seitz's use of light sources available on set was considered innovative in 1950, the shot in which Joe reads Norma's screenplay while Max brings a lamp over to him being regarded by Herb Lightman in *American Cinematographer* as "source lighting carried to the ultimate degree."[10] Typically for Wilder, the filming is always in thrall to the screenplay. As Max tells Joe that there are no locks in the house, a whip pan shows us each lockless door, while the film's gloomy fades remind us that this is the story of a dead man.

Sinyard and Turner succinctly describe the film's intermingling of genres, from film noir to *March of Time*-style urban documentary, with an overlay of Gothic horror. Arguably, the proposed opening scene (in which Joe is brought into the morgue on Friday afternoon and proceeds to tell the other occupants his story), is reminiscent in tone of the Bellevue Hospital sequence in another Wilderian generic hybrid *The Lost Weekend*. However, the beauty of *Sunset Blvd.* is its balance, a balance which such a preface, by tipping the film further into the macabre, would have fatally distorted.

Great filmmakers do not simply take the genres and conventions governing them and fill them with their own preoccupations. They develop them so that others must acknowledge and negotiate them in order to move on. *Sunset Blvd.* led Hollywood from the pre-war era to the post-war era. Having witnessed the human devastation of the pre-war world on his tour of duty with the Armed Forces in 1945, Wilder could no longer acquiesce in the cozy solutions offered by pre-war Hollywood. Indeed, for Andrew Sarris, in Joe's regret over living at such cost to himself and others are reverberations of the Holocaust itself. But, in trading in the changes which Hollywood weathered on the level of film content and production methods between 1927 and 1950, the film looks with awe at the molding of the industry's technical and generic conventions, and looks forward to the changed industrial structures from which Wilder would benefit, and further to the dizzy generic reworkings of today. When the film was previewed for the industry, Louis B. Mayer, head of MGM and probably the most powerful figure in the industry at the time, scorned Wilder for biting the hand that was feeding him. If *Double Indemnity* dared suggest that middle-class neighborhoods were not all cozy, and *The Lost Weekend* dared suggest that alcoholism was a disease and not a joke, *Sunset Blvd.* militated against the very institutions responsible for propagating such myths. In his next project, Wilder turned on "those heartless so-and-sos" in the newspaper business.

Barbara Stanwyck is said to have repeatedly kissed the hem of Swanson's garment at that preview. Given the realistic tradition out of which the actor had emerged, she might more appropriately have kissed the hem of Olson's.

6

Ace in the Hole

In 1951 Wilder made a film which not only embarrassed Hollywood, but offended America. Financially, it was far from successful, and if Paramount needed an excuse to shelve it, they had one. Only in Europe did it find a following, being shown at the Venice Film Festival and subsequently becoming a favorite among film study groups and in Wilder retrospectives.

In an effort to mitigate the scalding tone of this attack on gutter journalism and the ethics of the herd, Paramount — much to Wilder's annoyance — changed its title to *The Big Carnival*. There is an industry notion that the adjective "Big" somehow signifies to the audience that the film it has paid to see will be a crime movie, such titles as *The Big Sleep* and *The Big Clock* having proven big successes at the box office. But while *The Big Carnival* was banned in Singapore for its unsavory portrait of American life, *Ace in the Hole* won an award at Venice. This unblinking account of a journalist's unscrupulous attempt to rescue his career is quite the most grubby Wilder film of his early period. Of the failure of its brutal realist aesthetic, Wilder has said that "Audiences expected a cocktail and felt I was giving them a shot of vinegar instead."[1]

Sunset Blvd. marked the end of the Wilder and Brackett screenwriting partnership. Given their apparent personal incompatibility, it is hard to imagine how they could have written 13 screenplays together. Brackett, a conservative Republican and ex–*New Yorker* drama critic, must have seemed more than a little staid to the racy, risk-taking Wilder, and accounts of the partnership are peppered with their creative clashes. In retrospect, the break seemed inevitable, given Wilder's drift towards ever more controversial subjects from the mid–1940s onwards. It is easy to picture Brackett honing the gentle innuendoes of *The Major and the Minor* or the "meet-cute" in *The Lost Weekend*. Wilder's tastes, on the other hand, increasingly reflected a modernity which deviated more and more from the etiquette of a '30s Hollywood boudoir. *Ace in the Hole* is closer to the passion and anger of Stroheim's *Greed* than to the acerbic humor of Lubitsch's *Ninotchka*.

Co-written with Walter Newman (later to be acclaimed for hard-hitting drama *The Man with the Golden Arm* and western spoof *Cat Ballou*), and ex-journalist Lesser Samuels, ex-journalist Wilder could appreciate the spell which a man trapped underground would have for journalist Chuck Tatum (Kirk Douglas) and the implications for the society which came to watch.

Drawing on a fascination with the crazy American 1920s which was fueled in Vienna and would fuel at least two of Wilder's best films, the plot was prompted by the Kentucky cave-in which buried Floyd Collins for 18 days in 1925. The event attracted such nationwide attention that the journalist on the spot won the Pulitzer Prize, a fact not lost on Wilder's ambitious protagonist.

Ace in the Hole is a disturbing film. It is complex because the failure of Tatum's scheme to keep Leo Minosa (Richard Benedict) buried while he drums up media interest paradoxically leaves Wilder's audience vaguely disappointed. As America rolls up, big Buicks and Plymouths kicking up a moral haze as Tatum implicates the crowd in his design, Wilder is implicating us in Tatum's audacity. Tatum is another of Wilder's hard-boiled Americans whose straitened circumstances tempt them to work the system, whatever the cost. Walter Neff's cocky resilience makes crooking the insurance industry almost a legitimate career challenge. Joe Gillis is driven to exploit a situation which practically falls in his lap. The prospect of Harry Hinkle's reconciliation with his ex-wife in *The Fortune Cookie* blinds him to the ethical squalor of his brother-in-law's scheme. Wilder has great sympathy for those Americans who subvert their apparently entrepreneurial birthright by contriving schemes as scams. Their bravado is irresistible, Tatum's "Now that they've pitched me a big one, I'm gonna smack it right out of the ballpark" colorfully announcing his subscription to a philosophy all too familiar in the second half of the century. As Stephen Farber has elaborated in *Film Comment*, such characters are artists, planning and executing their designs with the finesse of sculptors and the chutzpah of confidence tricksters.

In a film in which Tatum is on screen practically throughout, he becomes the author of the film's events, a journalist whose embellishment of facts unites him with Wilderian fiction mongers Don Birnam and Joe Gillis. As Gillis says, "Audiences don't know that someone sits down and writes a picture. They think the actors make it up as they go along." If Tatum has invented Leo's ordeal, the audience goes along with it. The scenario which he has crafted is also a fictional analogy of the controlled experiment wrought by Wilder in making the film. Pulling off his scheme is for Tatum as important as pulling off the entertainment was for Wilder. Sinyard and Turner summarize the film's resonances: "The accident spot is transformed into a kind of surrogate cinema — a drive-in to which the masses are drawn … to witness a literal life and death struggle. The cars line up in orderly rows, just as people sit in theaters, their attention focused on the mountain. The spatial relationship between the viewer and the screen is precisely echoed, and to the thousands of spectators the drama on the mountain must resemble a movie … Wilder frequently cuts between the action and the audience…. Audiences of *Ace in the Hole* and the film's sponsors must have been aware of this implied criticism — especially Paramount, whose famous mountain logo assumes an ironic significance in this context — and reacted accordingly."[2]

For Brackett, *Ace in the Hole* arose out of the muckraking tradition of American letters. "It was in the vein of American self-criticism which has been a major current in our national literature since the days of The *Octopus* and *The Pit* and *The Jungle*."[3] The muck which Wilder raked was a certain tendency among the so-called "Great American Public," here exemplified by the Federbers (Frank Cady and Geraldine Hall), whose stop at Escudero (ironically) for its "instructive" possibilities. The Federbers are the inane spokespeople for a swirling mass "that moves when told, buys when beckoned, sings when prompted, leaves when dismissed."[4] Without his audience, Tatum's enterprise would have no consensus to endorse it. Just as without his, Wilder would have no consensus to endorse *Ace in the Hole*. Because "bad news sells best," and Tatum has the will to make it happen, there is a public ravenous enough to buy. It is as much voyeurism as artistry which has enabled his conceit, the Federbers expressing more concern to be remembered as the first to set up camp than for a man who is dying of pneumonia. If Wilder (and we) half admires Tatum, Wilder (and Tatum) has nothing but contempt for the muggy air of self-service which attends Leo's wife Lorraine (Jan Sterling), and the crowds who buy her burgers.

Amidst the stagnant air of New Mexico, we can appreciate displaced New Yorker Tatum's longing to break with the *Albuquerque Sun-Bulletin*. In a striking ellipsis, Wilder conveys the passage of a year's tenure in a single dissolve. Tatum strides towards the camera until he blocks out the light (as he will for Leo), before striding away with his perennial complaint to his inert colleagues. Wilder's America is invariably urban, his sterile New Mexico foreshadowing the diminished possibilities of "Climax, Nevada" in *Kiss Me, Stupid*. Tatum's complaint is a tribute to absent metropolitan delights: "no chopped chicken livers, no garlic pickles, no Lindy's, no Madison Square Garden, no Yogi Berra, no subway smelling sweet and sour, no chic little dames across a crowded bar ... AND WHAT DO YOU USE FOR NOISE AROUND HERE!" While a map of the "Land of Enchantment" hangs whimsically on the wall behind his desk, insulting Tatum's intelligence but obliquely foretelling his downfall, it is easy to appreciate the allure of post-war New York for Leo and Lorraine, its promise racily embodied in Tatum.

Indeed, it is Tatum whom the crowd comes to see, not Leo, dying invisibly in the cave. As the camera meekly follows his prowl around the office, these soporific New Mexicans are sucked deep into his discontent. Even his unorthodox arrival, in a convertible with burned-out bearings hitched to a pickup truck, seems to focus attention on Tatum. Comparison can be found here with Joe Gillis' "disabled" arrival at Norma's stifling backwater. Not only are both writers down on their luck, but both are worldly characters about to encounter innocents briefly empowered by their coming. For all his immorality, Tatum is the only character in *Ace in the Hole* who seems to be alive. The embroidered maxim — "TELL THE TRUTH" — on the office wall is a limp excuse for never saying or doing anything. Hustling versus lethargy is essential to the film's dichotomy between Civilization and the Wilderness, life and death. If for many an American director the small town has been a fount of virtue and common sense, for Wilder it is a pit of ennui and stupidity. If Tatum's arrogance is chilling, as McBride and Wilmington point out, "What is more chilling is that everyone lies down and plays dead before him."[5]

The only character who is prepared to argue the case for journalistic integrity is the *Sun-Bulletin*'s editor Jacob Boot (Porter Hall). Boot is the wizened descendent of such solid and self-evident heroes as Gary Cooper's Longfellow Deeds in the Capra comedy *Mr. Deeds Goes to Town*. He is a pre-war figure, his upstanding principles withered by the harsh air of the post-war world. But, if his belt-and-suspenders philosophy (making certain of everything he prints) seems archaic amid the fast-talking hustle of modern life, Tatum is seen wearing both at the point of his direst immersion in this stultifying atmosphere, intensifying our desire to see Tatum freed from the *Sun-Bulletin*.

Boot is an inadequate moral arbiter because he is too smug, his conservatism too ingrained for a world which is changing before him. When Tatum tells him that young Herbie Cook (Bob Arthur), the paper's apprentice and Tatum's sidekick, wants to get going careerwise, Boot's "Going where?" has an undeniable ring of reason, but so does Tatum's "What makes you think the *Albuquerque Sun-Bulletin* is all the kid wants out of life?" Tatum's scheme engenders our admiration because *Ace in the Hole* lacks another character with the presence to oppose him, Boot haunting the film like some spindly plague rather than standing effectively for an ethical position.[6] Even the law, represented by Sheriff Kretzer, a petty official with all the scruples of the rattlesnake he carries about with him, sides with Tatum so as to be reelected for appearing to do good by the entombed man.

The Eastern reporters who infest the press tent are brothers to the rats in *The Front Page*, Wilder's '70s reappraisal of the tabloid movie. Like Herbie, Lorraine, Kretzer and the crowd, they go along for the ride. For their acid portraits of the hard-nosed newshound, *Ace in the Hole* and *The Front Page* are films which leave the sourest aftertaste. The vision of professionals voraciously feeding from their own was too much for a section of the American press, and such was the outcry that Paramount sent press agents to every city desk in the land to convince editors that the film was not intended to attack journalism per se, just its bad apples.

Lorraine is sister to the opportunist Sandy in *The Fortune Cookie*. Rescued from a dive in Baltimore by a Leo who looked good in uniform, she has become heiress to an American Indian curio shack in the middle of nowhere. After five years in Escudero, she too is suffocating. All the more ironic, therefore, that Tatum will almost asphyxiate her with Leo's wedding anniversary present, a small fur piece, while Leo suffocates underground. As Mama Minosa prays, Lorraine slouches through the film until, windblown but dressed to kill, she hitches a lift as soon as the show is over. As Walter does for Phyllis, Lorraine hopes that Tatum can free her from a buried existence. Poorly educated and naive, Lorraine's options are as pathetic as the peroxide antiheroine's in *Double Indemnity*. Another victim of unrealistic marital expectations, she is unable to realize her potential without the wayward influence of a man. Taken in by Leo's promises of a spread out west, Lorraine, like

Chuck Tatum, American Journalist. Tatum (Kirk Douglas) tells Jacob Boot (Porter Hall) a thing or two about postwar tabloid aesthetics in *Ace in the Hole*.

Phyllis, neurotically repeats a pattern of behavior from which Tatum's scheme cannot save her, and which will ruin her life.

Nagel, editor of the *New York Daily* and Tatum's old boss, epitomizes the driven and corrupt "eastern" ethos embodied by Tatum and his cronies. Overplayed in hysterical style by Richard Gaines (the monoculous Norton in *Double Indemnity*), Nagel is so steeped in the mendacious end of the tabloid tradition that he cannot believe Tatum even when he owns up to his scam. The most damning moment in the film, at this point we realize that if no one prints the facts, there is no hope either for Tatum's soul or for Leo's memory. When he turns from Nagel's snub and asks Herbie if he believes him, Herbie's assent damns Herbie and Tatum both. Wilder is fond of surveying the dynamics of "buddy-buddy" relationships,[7] and Tatum's with his "fan" Herbie anticipates alliances ranging from novice Rudy Keppler's with Hildy Johnson in *The Front Page* to innocent Harry Hinkle's with conniving Willie Gingrich in *The*

Fortune Cookie. Herbie's fascination with the hard-drinking newspaper man is key for mediating our admiration for Tatum. In the drowsy *Sun-Bulletin* office, only these two seem to communicate. Herbie may never have been taught Tatum's methods of circulation-building at journalism college but, in this tired atmosphere he is, understandably, seduced by Tatum's dynamism.

Ace in the Hole has been read by Dick as a parodic reenactment of the story of Genesis. "We are back in the archetypal Garden ... an innocent Adam lies transfixed in a cave for six days, his Eve sinks her teeth into an apple ... the biblical serpent [is carried] around in a cardboard box. The imagery is ... mythic and unrelievedly ugly: ominous mountains, blowing dust, a snake rattling against cardboard...."[8]

Religion rarely features overtly in Wilder's films, but Dick's argument is persuasive. The analogy between the controlling axis of the film — Tatum/Wilder — and God creating the earth becomes the more vivid if we recall the sanctity of the screenplay for Wilder. Riding the crest of his first wave when *Ace in the Hole* was conceived and shot, the grounds for calling Wilder an auteur were never more sure than in 1950. The film's religious imagery — crosses on bare walls, candles, a Spanish church, an old Mexican woman silently praying — provide a stark contrast with the clamor of a restless journalist, an inconstant wife, and the fleeting crowd outside. All the more striking, in this respect, is the close-up of Tatum as the priest blesses the dying Leo. Once consumed with self-regard, Tatum is now consumed with self-disgust. As much in need of blessing as Leo, he has come full circle, the sanctity of a "human interest" story eclipsed by the sanctity of a human life.

This is not only a remade world in which, with a man dead, the truth, the original word of God, has been rewritten and spiced up for the tabloids, but one in which the rule of pagan law has been invoked. When Leo, driven to distraction by the drill pounding above him, yells "It's enough to wake up the dead," we are reminded that the breaking of any taboo, whether pagan, Christian or secular, has to be paid for. The "bad spirits" which Tatum writes about may, like Boot's integrity, be a thing of the past, but the spells which they let loose in this land of enchantment invite a denouement as pessimistic as *Double Indemnity*'s. When Smollett, the drilling contractor, tells Tatum that it is too late to save Leo, Tatum, naked from the waist up, seems uncharacteristically vulnerable. However rare religious imagery may be in Wilder's work, the growing self-awareness and attempts at redemption undertaken by Walter Neff, Chuck Tatum and even Phyllis Dietrichson offer ample evidence that he believes in the ebb and flow of good and bad in people. Our identification with Tatum is reinforced by his emerging friendship with Leo. If he began by using Leo, he did so in the sincere belief that Leo too had something to gain by it. Like Herbie, Leo is Tatum's partner, and the pair will benefit mutually from Tatum's scheme. When Lorraine reminds him that Tatum likes those rocks burying Leo just as much as she does, a tiny cloud of self-knowledge crosses his face. When he talks to the doctor about Leo's chances, part of him needs to know that Leo has a tough constitution because, in spite of the self-serving logic of the scheme, he has grown closer to the trapped man.

His concern is underlined when he makes Lorraine wear Leo's present, not merely because it looks good for the story to have a dutiful wife at hand, but because Tatum realizes that she should have some respect for the man whom she married and who has kept her, and now lies dying. Tatum's fetching Leo a priest and telling the drooling crowd that the show is over, is an announcement that, although too late for both Leo and Tatum, he has at last reached a proper awareness of his place in the scheme of things. Having been driven to prioritize among a set of imperatives, the most desperate being that he has reached the bottom in his profession in a society in which the individual must stand alone or fail miserably, it is hugely ironic that Tatum now stands alone before the crowd, his scheme having failed, and yet reclaims something of his humanity.

Although steeped in the neo-realistic vein of a number of American thrillers of the period, *Ace in the Hole* also anticipates the best of '50s widescreen compositions. Charles Lang's high wide shot of a fresco of cars glinting in the sun foresees the fabulous panoramas of David Lean, a director Wilder has long admired. Overall, the shooting style has the unfussy look of straight reportage, a tendency which savagely undermines the contrivance on display.

The most acid of Wilder's experiments in realism, the aesthetic is stronger in *Ace in the Hole* than in any of his films so far. Shot in and around Gallup, New Mexico, as the film begins, plain white credits roll in the dust, proclaiming its vision of a humanity at its most soiled. Tatum and Herbie's arrival at the mountain is marked by swirling dust, sagebrush, and the interminable desert glare. When they meet Papa Minosa, Herbie comments that he looks like someone in a photograph of a mine disaster, characterizing him as an authentic victim of a real-life drama. With Hugo Friedhofer's doleful background music, and its Catholic resonance, *Ace in the Hole* straddles the parochial worlds of a

Grierson documentary and Italian neo-realism. However, as usual, Wilder has his agenda and Tatum constantly dominates the frame. In the shot in which he grips Lorraine's hair, his fist seems to blot out everything. The final shot, back at the *Sun-Bulletin*, is a low angle recording Tatum's tottering collapse, leaking blood (like Walter Neff) after Lorraine has stabbed him, and poetically reiterating his domination of the film, this time from the floorboards.

In poker parlance, an "ace in the hole" means a good hand, a fleeting pleasure which, like the movies are for many, is the most important thing in the world. With a pugnacity reminiscent of the young James Cagney, Douglas puts the world on the front page and the world can't resist. As '50s radio personality Bob Bumpas delivered Tatum's story to every suburb in the Southwest, Wilder's critique of American enterprise resounded in the boondocks.

7

Stalag 17

"Despite its setting, *Stalag 17* is really an exuberantly dispatched allegory of American consumerist society,"[1] or so ran the blurb in the National Film Theater (NFT) program at the time of the NFT's Wilder season in 1979. Despite its setting, this German prisoner-of-war camp "somewhere on the Danube" is not as important as the story of American heroism which takes place there. After the commercial failure of *Ace in the Hole*, this raucous 1953 comedy reconfirmed Wilder's commercial acumen; it was one of his most successful films.

"Who are we to argue with a hero?" Sergeant J. J. Sefton (William Holden) snipes at Lieutenant Dunbar (Don Taylor), a new prisoner fresh from single-handedly blowing up a German ammunition train. At the heart of *Stalag 17* is a startling reversal which sees antihero Sefton formulate, engineer and execute the first successful escape plan since anyone in Barrack 4 became a POW.

Like Wilderian antiheroes before him, Sefton is not the character we expect him to be. Self-styled camp black marketeer, for most of the film this "big-time operator" is serving himself in a wartime context which in many another film has amounted to selflessness and solidarity. But ever since arriving at Stalag 17 and being robbed of everything, he has attended only to his own interests. Whenever his peers concoct a fresh escape plan, he sarcastically enquires: "Did you calculate the risk?" questioning the efficiency of their plans and interrogating the rhetoric of loyalty and group cohesion so traditionally integral to the war movie. It is a position with which Wilder is in sympathy. While Sefton is partly disliked because he is suspected of informing on escapees and

J.J. Sefton, American Realist, *left to right,* **J.J. (William Holden) tells Hoffy (Richard Erdman), Price (Peter Graves), Duke (Neville Brand), and Feldwebel Schulz (Sig Rumann) a little something about the market economy in** *Stalag 17.*

so casually argues with conventional heroism, Sefton's peers object to him not so much out of loyalty to that noble cause, but mainly because he is such a smart businessman and, as a result, lives a relatively comfortable life. Providing an often amusing and sad backdrop to the film's main thrust, the discovery and revelation of Barrack 4's German informer, Sefton's peers are an often stupid and frequently vindictive mob.

Like other Wilderian antiheroes, even Sefton turns out to have a heroic streak, freeing Dunbar (even if only for the $10,000 reward he expects from Dunbar's rich parents), and offering the boys the hope that escape is a possible option. But, more importantly for film history, this eleventh-hour redemption elevates the smug Sefton by redefining the notion of the war movie hero itself. Eight years after the war ended, *Stalag 17* is less concerned with propaganda and more with the conventions which propelled it. In the pragmatic Sefton, Wilder and Edwin Blum's screenplay demonstrates that escaping from a German lager during World War II was less a question of brawn, endurance, and a few brains, and more a question of brains, endurance, and a little brawn. What *Stalag 17*'s screenplay acknowledges is that the average Nazi lager was an extremely well-organized machine for incarceration, one which would require an extremely well-organized plan to overcome. Countering the mindless heroics of many a wartime war movie, as well as the misty-eyed rhetoric of such as Wilder's own *Hold Back the Dawn* and *Five Graves to Cairo*, Sefton's American know-how anticipates the craftsman-escapees of future war films like Robert Bresson's *A Man Escaped* and John Sturges' *The Great Escape*. The thoughtful implication of *Stalag 17* is that the war was won by countering one fiendish design, be it escape plan, new offensive, or secret weapon, with an even more fiendish, in this case American-built, design. In the 50s, a decade of American commercial and cultural dominance, such an implication would also have carried a piquant economic edge.

As though to emphasize Sefton's enterprising spirit, much of *Stalag 17* consists of humorous but inconsequential vignettes. Relating this series of barrack room shenanigans and clockwork Nazi reprisals, Sefton's confederate Cookie's (Gil Stratton, Jr) voice-over narration feels like a series of *Boy's Own* comic anecdotes. The serious business of waging war is always elsewhere. At one point, the boys try to catch the BBC on their mock-up radio, but the sites of the German offensive in the Ardennes — Bastogne, Malmedy — seem like names in a history book rather than places which share the same world with the men. True to Wilder's journalistic penchant for revisiting old news, the episode nevertheless reiterates their isolation from a Europe where the action is. What provides the real substance of Cookie's narration is the story of how Sefton overturned everyone's opinion of him, caught the real informer, and escaped.

The vignettes — "Animal" and Harry plot road markings in order to get to the Russian women's delousing shed; the boys spy on the shed through Sefton's mock-up telescope; the Red Cross man pays his annual visit; the barracks have their Christmas parties — lend the film the mood of a TV series. In this deftly-turned set of episodes, Wilder tells funny stories about a familiar bunch whose tragedy was that they did nothing special during the war. Cookie charts a seemingly endless cycle of put-downs. The boys' every stab at heroism is undermined. At one point they are filling in their escape tunnel on the orders of the camp Oberst, and past them rolls a wagon carrying the coffins of Manfredi and Johnson, mown down as they tried to escape. The radio which they meticulously build reports nothing but bad news. Mimicking the shape of wartime Allied fortunes historically, it is a long time before the tide starts to turn.

This catalogue of pathos renders Sefton's coup all the more meaningful, as well as rendering thrilling what has been a rather static and talky film. The episodes have a cut-and-dried air which is reflected in the limitations of their protagonists. The crashing irony of *Stalag 17* is that the character who has been deemed cut-and-dried by the other prisoners turns out to be a hero, if not a patriot. As a pragmatic entrepreneur with know-how to spare, Sefton is, arguably, the most typically "American" of all the POWs. In common with *Double Indemnity*, *Stalag 17* is detective film in which Sefton is always one step ahead of the others because he knows that he is not the informer, yet there is an informer. Rather than merely deny the second premise, his position pushes him uniquely nearer to knowing who that informer is. Clearly, Barrack 4 is in dire need of Sefton's logical nature.

His accusers are the "camp clowns" "Animal" (Robert Strauss) and Harry Schapiro (Harvey Lembeck). A self-styled double-act for the diversion of the other prisoners, (and the amusement of Wilder's audience until outstripped by Sefton's performance), "Animal" is a brawny unshaven retard in long johns, alive only to the smell of food and a pin-up of Betty Grable. Harry is his Jewish stooge. In an ineffectual reversal of the Sefton-Cookie relationship, the "fixer" Harry promises to ply "Animal" with women and food. "Sometimes I'm so sharp it's frightening," he tells his friend, but, like unfortunate screenwriter Joe Gillis, Harry is down seven payments on his Plymouth and the finance company is closing in. In one of the most shattering deceptions in a film with its fair share of Wilderian duplicity, he masquerades as Betty Grable at the barrack Christmas party. When he realizes that he has been dancing not with the woman of his dreams but with his best friend, the drunken "Animal" is beside himself with disappointment. In this forerunner of the Wilder cross-dressing classic *Some Like It Hot*, Wilder begins to explore the pain and loneliness which underlies many of his "buddy-buddy" arrangements. Harry's impotence (and, by extension, that of all the prisoners) becomes glaringly obvious when, during a volleyball game, he relieves a German guard of his rifle so that he can join in, but lacks wit or morale to exploit this stroke of luck.

Duke (Neville Brand, a noted '50s heavy) is a one-dimensional thug who can only simmer with resentment whenever Sefton is around. The appropriately-named Price (Peter Graves) is the tall, blond, blue-eyed barrack security officer and barrack spy, informing the Germans of every escape attempt. If this were another war film, this chess-playing WASP would be the barrack hero. Here he is just a rather over-privileged shifty-eyed traitor. Hoffy acts only as the necessary efficient-seeming barrack chief, his efficiency constantly undermined by Price.

Indulging in idle rituals and reacting mechanically to the demands which their incarceration creates, none of these characters have the ability to think for themselves. Steeped in their ennui, they are like the mediocre crowd in *Ace in the Hole*, streaming past the telescope to watch the Russian women, jumping when mail or food is distributed, accusing Sefton of betraying them when they have nothing better to do. Only Joey, the brain-damaged mute with his mournful ocarina, pays some slight homage to Sefton's intelligence by smiling to himself when Price is thrown into the compound as a decoy. Joey was present when Sefton surreptitiously cross-examined Price about his background and, earlier, Sefton had given him half of his fried egg. It is an exchange which reveals depths in the two men which have been smothered by the thoughtless clamor of barrack life. Sporting a baseball cap, seemingly the richest flyer's jacket in the camp, and a cigar clamped between his teeth, the chipper American Sefton is a lonely and mistreated reflection of the degraded men around him. When he gains conclusive evidence of what we already know, (that Price is the informer) the sense of released outrage is deeply satisfying.

Dunbar's confederate Bagradian (Jay Lawrence) entertains the boys with impressions of movie stars, reinforcing the sense in which they are cut off from "Civilization." Significantly, he is also the unofficial keeper of the history of Dunbar's heroic exploits, playing the same narrational role as Cookie does vis-à-vis Sefton. Although a small role, Bagradian is a key character in a film devoted to the demolition of conventional stereotypes. After all his legend-mongering, it is down to Sefton-the-Stoolie to save Dunbar-the-Hero, as well as rid Barrack 4 of the real stoolie. As Leland Poague describes it,[2] dramatically *Stalag 17* is a cautionary tale about characters who leap to conclusions about their own infallibility — Price/Hoffy and Co/Scherbach — and the fallibility of others. Metaphorically, it is a cautionary tale about people who leap to conclusions about heroic stereotypes and star images. Extending Wilder's meditation upon the illusory nature of cinema begun in *Hold Back the Dawn*, *Stalag 17* cautions America against another outbreak of the recent scourge of McCarthyism.

"It always makes me sore when I see those war pictures, all about flying leathernecks and submarine patrols and frog men and guerrillas in the Philippines. What gets me is that there never was a movie about POWs, about prisoners of war." Cookie's complaint announces that Wilder's film is no ordinary war picture. While the wealthy Bostonian Dunbar has all the right connections, he turns out to have little of the right stuff when being interrogated by Oberst von Scherbach (Otto Preminger),[3] a cardboard German officer whose sarcasm easily demolishes Dunbar. Expert in the arts of resource management and strategic planning, the lower middle-class Sefton does have the right stuff, including a stout pair of wire-cutters, plenty of cigarettes, and a brain. In a sly dig at the ineffectual men of Barrack 4, and at his own failed Lubitschian musical *The Emperor Waltz*, Wilder has Sefton pick up an Alpine cap much like that worn by Bing Crosby in the earlier film and retort, "I'll look pretty stupid in this, yodeling my way across the Alps."

As Sinyard and Turner have observed, Dunbar's crippled unheroic state when Sefton rescues him from his icy water tank refuge reinforces his status as an object, a commodity which Sefton is well used to handling. Sefton's climactic exposure of Price, followed by his plan to rescue Dunbar and flee Stalag 17, constitutes a feat of organization a million miles from the schoolboy heroics of the other men. Indeed, in contrast with the episodic plotting of the film's first half, Sefton's plan unwinds like one of Wilder's tightly-plotted films. Like Joe Gillis and Chuck Tatum's, Sefton's materialism is an understandable response to a milieu in which all are dreamers. Like them, Sefton redeems his less worthy acts by pulling the wool from the eyes of those around him. He may not respect these "comrades" who have scorned him, but he does free them from the traitor who has dogged their escape attempts, leaving him free and them a little wiser.

If the protagonists of *Double Indemnity*, *Sunset Blvd.* and *Ace in the Hole* inhabit metaphorical prisons, here the prison is suffocatingly real. Like the franchise operators of *Ace in the Hole*, only Sefton turns a profit and can leave when he wants. The claustrophobic sets of *Stalag 17* never admit to a world beyond their confines, only to a muddy yard as confining as the barracks. Ostensibly set in Europe, the war experiences which brought the men to Stalag 17 are never discussed, while their pastimes — a "Kentucky Derby" rat race, a volleyball game, a procession to the strains of *When Johnny Comes Marching Home*— are determinedly American.

With remarkable piquancy, Wilder and Blum play with the collision between German and American English in this cramped environment, creating a bantering patois between the boys and Feldwebel Schulz

(Sig Rumann)[4] which constitutes both a rebellion against their German overlords and a colorful commentary upon the position of a "German" directing Americans. War movie German could never be taken seriously after "Animal's" barking "Raus!" Preposterous German ideologies are demolished with gleeful American élan when copies of *Mein Kampf* are distributed among the men, prompting a mass impersonation of Hitler which sees Wilder at his playful best.

In keeping with its claustrophobic mood, *Stalag 17* begins with a tracking shot of a German guard and an Alsatian patrolling at the cramped foot of a high wire fence while the plain white "packing crate"–type credits which began *Sunset Blvd.* announce the film's impoverished naturalistic milieu. Shot so as to exploit the drabbest hues of the monochrome spectrum, *Stalag 17* has hardly a stylistic flourish. Like the environment, the film feels spartan, Ernest Laszlo's camera finding no opportunity for fluid movement. Wilder overcomes this by exploiting the depth of focus which the long barrack room affords, and the film is full of scenes which draw attention away from the frame itself, inviting us to look into the frame as a composition. Notice when a voice comments upon events in the foreground, our attention is drawn to the grizzled face of "Animal" in the background, both planes in focus. When Sefton discovers that Price is the informer, the camera follows Price away from the carousing men in the background, keeping both in focus until the barrack chess table appears, at which point there is a cut. Price then swaps the black queen with a message in it for an identical piece. The long take which takes him from the bunk near the men where he started resumes as he wanders back and joins the emerging procession. Wilder then cuts to Sefton as he notices that the shadow of the light bulb cord behind him hangs straight as opposed to looped — a signal that the swap has been made. The cuts economically illustrate the disconnection between Price and the men he is betraying, and between Sefton and the men who ostracize him, uniting informer and suspected informer.

The failure of the men to cohere as a group is emphasized by Wilder's framing of them solitarily or in two-shots as couples. Following mail call, Laszlo's camera goes on a tour of the bunks as each man reads his letters. Indeed, the predicament of men incarcerated while their women roam is no more painfully suggested than by the prisoner who wistfully, then frantically, tries to persuade himself, first by talking to a friend and then in a frame to himself, that the baby left on his wife's doorstep is not truly her own. We are reminded of duplicitous war widow Phyllis Dietrichson. Outside, the men tramp through snow and mud, atomized in their search for scraps as they are in Primo Levi's account of Auschwitz, *If This Is a Man*, while indoors each is confined to a single bunk. As it will in *The Apartment*, the fact that the action takes place over the last week before Christmas emphasizes the want of solidarity.

Wilder's respect for the dramatically loaded object also reinforces *Stalag 17*'s spartan feel. Sefton's revelation and redemption turns upon a light bulb and a chess piece. Joey's ocarina, when thrown into a puddle so as to splash von Scherbach, becomes a symbol of the men's rebellion. Elsewhere, "Animal" and Harry drool over an egg prepared by Sefton for his breakfast. As he cracks it open, slides it around the pan, tosses it into the air, we too begin to drool. In this deprived world, the luxuries of life back home take on a mystical status. It is a phenomenon which *The Seven Year Itch* will explore in breathtaking fashion.

8

The Seven Year Itch

The Seven Year Itch is not among the best of Wilder's films, although it has improved with the years. Wilder himself felt that its slight narrative would have benefited had mid–1950s mores allowed married man Tom Ewell to bed his shapely neighbor Marilyn Monroe. As in the past, the European view has been kinder. In 1975 FrançoisTruffaut wrote: "It doesn't take seven minutes to realize that *The Seven Year Itch* is beyond smut and licentiousness and that it takes us past the limits of evil to a kind of worn-down regret, good humor, and kindness."[1] Its worn-down regret, the warmth felt by the irrevocably married Richard Sherman, and that felt by the fun-loving Girl, each for the other, constitutes the charming essence of a film which toys with the sexual possibilities of a revolution which by 1955 was already on the horizon.

The Seven Year Itch is based upon George Axelrod's successful 1952 Broadway play and was co-written by Axelrod and Wilder. His first film away from Paramount, with whom Wilder's association since *Ace in the Hole* had grown increasingly strained, the deal signed with 20th Century–Fox made Wilder co-producer as well as co-writer. It also obliged him to cast the studio's (and America's) biggest star as the Girl. *The Seven Year Itch* was Fox's biggest hit of that year. Yet it lacks the clarity of other Wilder films. This is perhaps because Wilder was working at an unfamiliar studio and with an unfamiliar writer (despite shared themes), whose own work they were adapting. The overall impression is of a Wilderian comedy compromised by other hands.

The screenplay's premise springs from pseudo-psychological territory which Wilder has taken delight in satirizing. According to the treatise which pulp novelette executive Sherman is planning to adapt, the "Seven Year Itch" is the tendency among husbands in the seventh year of marriage to commit adultery in order to savor what they have been missing. As a premise for a sex comedy, this works well. But this is Axelrod territory, and the writer's perennial interest lies in telling commentaries on the evolution of the American male libido. What characterizes the civilized male American outlook in the post-war period is an inability to reconcile a liberal-humanist view of the American female with a historical desire to appropriate her sexually. Such a desire found endorsement in the publication of the Kinsey Report in 1948–1953, demonstrating that sexual practices hitherto regarded as perversions were actually widespread. The Report was influential in an increase of sexual permissiveness.

Sherman's failure to act on his desire for the Girl is typical. "Axelrod comes close to defining the post–Kinsey, pre–Reichian male who has become aware of sexual alternatives to which neither Hollywood nor society would let him respond — except with brittle wisecracks, bashful leers, and bleeding ulcers,"[2] wrote Richard Carliss. But if this failure to act leaves a vacuum at the film's core, it is filled, at least notionally, by Sherman's recognition that sexual possibilities may be many in this plentiful land, but individuals are here not only for the purposes of hungry appropriation.

Having both the perception of a child and the savvy of an adult, the Girl recognizes that Sherman embarks upon his habitual imaginings because he is lonely without his wife. What his charming wife Helen (Evelyn Keyes) realizes is that his imagination is part of his charm: "You read too many books and see too many movies." Left to fend for himself during a sweltering New York summer while Helen and son Ricky are on holiday in Maine, Sherman is conditioned by the overwrought fictions which he markets to channel his loneliness into overwrought daydreams. Missing Helen's warmth and companionship, and laboring under the dietary restrictions imposed by his doctors, Sherman becomes drawn to the voluptuous Girl upstairs.

His malaise expresses itself in indecision. He is torn by conflicting scenarios — Helen thinks he has slept with the Girl; Helen trusts him; Helen is on her way home; Helen is enjoying herself with Tom Mackenzie — and conflicting perceptions of himself. Like Don Birnam, he must get through this period of abstinence and confront the ghastly spectre of his weak alter ego. As there are two Dons, "Don the drunk and Don the writer," so there are two Richards. One is normal, one is instinctual, like the twin visages in *The Picture of Dorian Gray*, whose vicious "other" Sherman imagines he sees in his own mirror reflection. After making an abortive pass at the Girl, he apologizes: "The only excuse I can possibly offer is that I'm not myself." Birnam and Sherman are well aware of the essential duality of their characters. But while its consequences are grave for Birnam, for Sherman they only seem to be. Lacking the drive to become a writer himself, Sherman is, nevertheless, wracked by the choices which his perceptions present. And so he impotently imagines.

Whereas in Wilder films like *The Lost Weekend* and *Ace in the Hole*, the protagonists act and create their respective downfalls, Axelrod protagonists like Sherman and Stanley Ford in the Axelrod-scripted *How to Murder Your Wife* (1964) merely imagine such an event. Arguably, the desire under which Sherman labors is not for the Girl but truly for Helen. "I'm probably the most married man you'll ever know," he assures the Girl (and himself). After a fantasy in which he seduces her to a Rachmaninov piano concerto, his "I'm afraid that wasn't such a good idea" is an admission that clichés don't work between men and women but spontaneity will. What is funny about Sherman's malaise are the tensions which it highlights between models of behavior and that which real situations demand. Sherman is trapped for most of the film in a perception of the situation which leads from mistrust to melodrama as his feelings get the better of him. While for the Girl, it is most fun when things are simply allowed to happen. Ultimately, Sherman's fears about himself are as insubstantial as the cool air which famously sends the Girl's skirt billowing over her head on Lexington Avenue. While Sherman, never a mover and a shaker himself, merely looks on. It is a moment which perhaps encapsulates the difference between Axelrod's life of the mind and the Wilderian life of action.

In this conservative Hollywood comedy it is necessary that Sherman not sleep with the Girl because, if he did, the yearning for female warmth (Helen's warmth) would be dissipated. From such a scenario, Sherman would emerge a sated Lothario dashing guiltily off to find his wife. In the film, the vision of dopey Sherman haphazardly dashing out of the apartment is unequivocal. He has nothing to hide from Helen, and everything to offer her. Arguably, Sherman's indecision from the moment when Helen and Ricky board the train is nothing more than a series of reactions serving eminently well the risqué demands of the genre. It is generically necessary for the Girl to be abundantly around because, as Norman Mailer writes, "In the Eisenhower years, comedy resides in how close one can come to the concept of hot pussy while still living in the cool of the innocent."[3]

As Richard Corliss puts it, if the men in Axelrod's comedies are "Middle-Aged Apollonian Pygmalions," his women are young "Dionysian Galateas."[4] The Girl (unnamed, significantly) is little more than a sex object in an overworked imagination. Paradoxically, it is precisely because of the Girl's substantial physical presence that Helen can be excused for taking her for a figment in her lonely husband's mind. For Truffaut, her looks even erode the film's potential as cinema. "On screen, there is no chance to reflect. Hips, nape, knees, ears, elbows, lips, palms of the hand, profiles win out over tracking shots, framing, sustained panoramas, dissolves."[5] This seems appropriate in a film which simultaneously celebrates and rues the material plenty which was America in the '50s. In this light, the Girl/Monroe comes to symbolize a glorious object-filled nirvana. Yet the function of the Girl is to be what Helen temporarily cannot be: mate to the American husband. By laughing at his jokes, marveling at his skills, and yearning for his maturity, the Girl is there to prop up his ego. She is simultaneously a beautiful object and a playmate. Offering affection rather than sex, the Girl represents the possibility of ownership while reserving a place for Helen — a more substantial presence still because she has a mind of her own.

Graham McCann describes the publicity campaign organized by Fox around Monroe as the Girl. "When her role was finalized, the studio assigned a 'unit man' to 'plant' items related to her and her role in the press; television appearances were discussed, interviews were arranged. New York publicity offices of the studio took over the campaign when the distribution-exhibition stage started; national advertising and merchandise tie-ins exploited the film's promise…. They had a gigantic blow-up of her *Seven Year Itch* pose positioned over a street."[6] Given the furious objectification of Monroe during this build-up, it is easy to see the film as a concentrated statement of Monroe's much-discussed predicament as an actress trying to be taken seriously, a woman longing to be an individual. Both she and Wilder are almost at a loss before a part consisting of trademark pouts and an innocence which, under the circumstances, seems ludicrous. This Galatea wished to live among mortals.

Wilder and Axelrod have in their respective ways both been interested in the fate of innocents in an uncaring world. Sherman has much in common with romantic spirit Don Birnam, deserted by *his* Helen for the weekend. Sherman also anticipates schnook-mensch C. C. Baxter in *The Apartment*. Sherman is too the archetypal Axelrod male; overawed by the consumer society and the pleasures which it apparently affords the individual. He anticipates Harold Lampson, Stanley's bewildered wife-dominated lawyer in *How to Murder Your Wife*.

Both *The Seven Year Itch* and *How to Murder Your Wife* share with the Axelrod-scripted *Breakfast at Tiffany's* (1961) a preoccupation with the predicament of the Hollywood project which wants to partake in the new sexual modernity of the '50s and '60s, but is afraid of interrogating the conventional happy ending. If *Breakfast at Tiffany's* revels in that party at Holly Golightly's East '70s brownstone (a mere few blocks from the Shermans' Gramercy Park apartment), where Holly lives out the sexual fantasy of the age, she will melt into the arms of the stable and promising young man upstairs. For a few short evenings, Sherman lives out the dream of the swinging bachelor, but eventually he flees to the boondocks of Maine where Helen faithfully waits. Sherman's fanciful designs on the Girl, Holly's sexual whirl and Stanley's bachelor lifestyle all make for a series of jokes and incidents which prolong the build-up to these films' respective blissful closures. All three films chart the progress of characters who, like the audience, are given time out to dream before resuming ordered lives. If Tiffany's is Holly's symbol of the world of plenty which was America in the post-war years, it is a world abundantly expressed in the brazen curves of Marilyn Monroe in *The Seven Year Itch*.

Wilder revels in the vulgarity of a character who dunks potato chips in champagne and recognizes classical music because it lacks a vocal. Along Lexington Avenue, the Girl, a model, plugs her latest assignment, a toothpaste commercial, unable even to converse without invoking the throwaway culture in which all America is immersed. The screenplay is rooted firmly in the rhetoric of the Affluent Society, its dialogue punctuated with the buzzwords of the era: "CinemaScope," stereophonic sound, "Dazzledent," co-axial cables, "Captain Video," the burgeoning health food craze. Here is the world which Wilder protagonists since Walter and Phyllis have longed to buy into. J. J. Sefton would have bought into this society as soon as he disembarked.

When the Girl tells Sherman that she plugged the tap with her big toe while trying to sleep in the bath on a hot night, he marvels at such native know-how. Only the Girl could keep her potato chips, her underwear, and a bottle of champagne in the icebox. Wilder himself marvels at this collision of high and low culture. Such a collision could only take place in America where there is plenty of everything and everything is game for consumption. At one point, the pair's monologues (his on the psychological "toboggan" on which all are doomed, hers on the logistics

Richard Sherman, American fantasist. Sherman (Tom Ewell) tries to figure out what makes America tick whilst the Girl (Marilyn Monroe) tries not to think about it in *The Seven Year Itch.*

of getting to sleep during a New York summer), converge with the question, "What are we going to do?" Such a question voices the dismay of little people swamped by an abundance of choice. It is the quandary of all individuals when rendered insignificant before the consumer society's insatiable demand. Both *The Seven Year Itch* and *Breakfast at Tiffany's* are partly about the sense in which these individuals are continually mired in a welter of choices — between products, partners, lifestyles. Both Sherman and Holly are shopping for possibilities. Both eventually settle for the solutions under their very noses.

The cornucopia extends throughout the dialogue. Alongside the advertising shorthand are the feverish adjectives of friend-of-the-family Tom Mackenzie's sexy best-sellers. In cheerful counterpoint, there is Sherman's homespun appeal in which are evoked "a flight of swallows winging their way back to Capistrano." Sherman's fantasies are couched in the hackneyed prose of bad movie dialogue, satirizing the efficient grind of the Hollywood factory celebrated in *Sunset Blvd.* No strand of production is exempt from the dialogue's ironizing glee, and contemporary movies ranging from prestige features like *From Here to Eternity* to *The Creature from the Black Lagoon* are ridiculed. Dr Brubaker's psychoanalytical babble, with its "dark clouds gathering on the psychic horizon," is lent a populist equivalent in janitor Kruhulik's leering "Summertime, and the livin' is easy." Yet this post-modern larding of allusion and irony tends to betray the fact that the action has nowhere to go. Sherman's pronouncements on classical music and psychology may find Wilder having fun at the expense of the acquisitive middle-class attitude towards knowledge and insight, but such screenplays as *The Lost Weekend* and *Sunset Blvd.* are allusive and ironic too. They are also lighter on their feet.

Although Jewish, and sensitive to the Jewish voices in his screenplays, Wilder was never quite part of that post-war Jewish-American literary culture to which such playwrights, novelists and screenwriters as Axelrod, Bellow and Allen belong. While Wilder has viewed psychoanalysis, that prime Jewish contribution to the age, as cerebral twaddle, these writers have welcomed Freud with open arms. However, Wilder and Axelrod have perhaps more in common than is immediately obvious. Axelrod is drawn to wish-fulfillment and the dream life. The pragmatist Wilder has little time for heroes too weak to act on their desires. Yet both writers are concerned with individual attempts to define themselves in the face of a monolithic society which consumes everything in its path. If this were Wilder's screenplay alone, Sherman would sleep with the Girl and inscribe his will on the society. But the film is as much

Axelrod's. So the real drama takes place beneath the glossy surface in the inattentions of a dynamic which constantly nags the man-child to act. We are primed from the start to expect the lonely husbands of New York to shake loose their civilized coils and enjoy a hootenanny.

While Brubaker's chapter—"The Repressed Urge in the Middle-Aged Male"—apparently offers lust its object, Brubaker himself apparently offers Sherman carte blanche to have his way with the Girl. At one point, Sherman picks up the phone, inadvertently answering "Hello, Mother." It is Helen. Such is the revealing helplessness into which her absence has plunged him. Helen is constantly nagging him to send Ricky his kayak paddle so that he can really enjoy himself. A strict Freudian would infer an Oedipal reading here. Elsewhere, Sherman gets his finger stuck in a champagne bottle. The dependence of these jokes on Freudian orthodoxy is rather more a premonition of the early sex-obsessed screenplays of Woody Allen[7] than an elaboration of Wilder's interest in sexual relations. Yet Sherman's claim as an imaginative artist is as valid as Don Birnam's or Walter Neff's. His claim as an individual is as valid as any Wilderian protagonist's.

Sherman's urge to fictionalize his life is the individual's response to a culture bent upon channeling desire into the dimensions of the consumable. What is touching about his dalliance with the Girl is that each gives rather than consumes. More genuinely romantic than the fantasies involving women he hardly knows, such as his secretary and a nurse, is Sherman's strolling through Manhattan with his neighbor on a summer evening to the gentle lilt of Alfred Newman's score. When she kisses him to prove "Dazzledent's" fresh breath confidence, the ad is sublimated by the act rather than the act being consumed in an ad. When Sherman returns the kiss, he returns a compliment which goes beyond the Middle-Aged leer. Shot against the backdrop of the real Lexington Avenue at two o'clock in the morning, the scene's mood looks forward to the devil-may-care scenes in which Holly and Paul partake of the resonant New York locations in *Breakfast at Tiffany's*. Softening Axelrod's Girl in order to fit her into Monroe's vulnerable mold, Wilder and the studio introduced a fetching sentimentality to the proceedings which increasingly discounts the film's broad innuendo. Wilder is always respectful of Monroe, discreetly shooting her from the knees down on Lexington Avenue, and yielding only once to a raunchy close-up of her backside when Sherman first sets eyes on her.

This warm center has the effect of distancing the viewer during Sherman's fantasies. Wilder may seamlessly pan-dissolve from reality to fantasy when Sherman embarks on another reverie, but these half-baked clichés look like the bad fiction they are when compared with his exchanges with the Girl. That in which he is seduced in a hospital bed looks like a scene from the TV series *Emergency Ward 10*. That in which he is seduced on a deserted beach is a parody of Fred Zinnemann's 1953 film *From Here to Eternity*. The fantasies dramatize the extent to which this overworked individual is trapped in a conformist lifestyle by enmeshing even his subjective life in a series of pre-packaged scenarios. Bad fiction counts for more than fact for Sherman. When he finally gets around to wrapping Ricky's paddle, he desperately tries to compensate for his imagined misconduct by imagining some more: "People send paddles every day. The mails are full of paddles." Sherman is in the throes of a rampant desire to fictionalize, not a rampant desire to seduce. When he punches Tom Mackenzie on the jaw we are reminded of another quirky Wilder fantasist, Orville Spooner, who ineffectually picks a fight with his wife in a later Wilder study of male insecurity—*Kiss Me, Stupid*.

There is a short scene which opens *The Seven Year Itch* shot at a New York rail terminal in which the announcer's voice reels off the New England destinations of the train now boarding. The scene has a vérité freshness about it which we have felt before in Wilder. But it is quickly lost amidst the gaudy allure of this big studio entertainment. The status of *The Seven Year Itch* as a Wilder film is undermined by 20th Century–Fox, keen to emboss the project with its "CinemaScope" widescreen and "DeLuxe" color treatment. The measure of studio hegemony is referred to when, in answer to Tom's question as to who is cooking in the Sherman kitchen, Sherman replies "Maybe it's Marilyn Monroe!" While Sherman's tentative discovery of his own humanity mirrors Monroe's beleaguered attempt to find herself as an actress in 1955, Wilder and Axelrod are engulfed by the economics of studio control. Wilder often shows the Girl and Sherman in duets of high and low-angle shots. We are back at the staircase separating Walter from Phyllis when they first meet. We are also reminded of the deity Galatea and the innocent Pygmalion. But, above all, the Girl is "MM," the studio's key screen goddess, consumable yet unattainable. With breasts like the brake lights on a Cadillac and a derriere as inviting as a triple cheeseburger, she is the epitome of the American dream of Abundance Declared, and the system which marketed it. If that system killed Joe Gillis and drove Norma Desmond insane, Wilder had to deal with it every day. As Axelrod has said of Hollywood: "Before, you were confronted with an illiterate, finagling, tyrannical guy who was very difficult to converse with, to convince, but once you did that job, that was it, you went ahead. But now there are *twenty* of those guys ... And then you find out after a year and a half that you have been kissing the wrong ass all along."[8]

Tom Ewell looks as though Frankenstein's monster had been rehabilitated and was living in a Manhattan duplex. Yet when he breaks into a cunning leer we know this to be the prerogative of a man itching to run amok and freed from having to keep up appearances. His solemnity at the piano, followed by an aristocratic "You came" as, expecting the Girl, he admits Kruhulik, wishing to replace a moth-eaten carpet, seems the measure of his detachment from reality and barely contains a manic intensity. Walter Matthau was Wilder's original choice for the role, and Ewell's old-shoe face clearly foresees the leering Matthau of *The Fortune Cookie* (1966) and *The Odd Couple* (1967).

Aside from securing the property for translation to the screen, Wilder's hand in casting around the principal roles is obvious. As usual, *The Seven Year Itch* contains a rich line-up of piquantly drawn Wilder background characters. Oscar Homolka's Dr. Brubaker is Wilder's revenge upon the Freud who ejected the young reporter from his house for presuming to request an interview. Robert Strauss' Kruhulik offers an only slightly more articulate version of his "Animal" of *Stalag 17*. In boater and silk tie, he is the epitome of the working-class immigrant son's notion of what it is to be a dapper American male. Doro Merande's health food restaurant waitress offers a real treat.

Richard Sherman is typical of the post-war American male as depicted in Jewish-American fiction and portrayed by such as Jack Lemmon and, later, Woody Allen. Before a figment of a culture intoxicated by largesse, Sherman is, like Wilder himself at 20th Century–Fox, engulfed by its totalitarian demand. Beset by fears about his wife, women in general, and especially himself, he needs not more commitments but the assurance that he is up to fulfilling those he already has. Like the '50s Abstract Expressionist aesthetic which Saul Bass' credits subvert, *The Seven Year Itch* is more than a Billy Wilder picture. It is a key artifact of a particular society at a particular stage in its evolution.

9

The Spirit of St. Louis

In a conversation with Maurice Zolotow, screenwriter Ernest Lehman said of Wilder: "As I got to know Billy, I was always surprised by how deeply he was immersed in American life. For instance, he isn't just a casual Dodger fan. He knows all the names and statistics and he feels the feelings that go with the names.... He feels like an American feels. I never think of Billy as being a European — not at all, not at all. You get Billy on a political subject, hell, he won't sound like a guy remote from the American scene. I have this feeling he was conscious of people thinking of him as European and I think he wanted to do *The Spirit of St. Louis* because it was a very American subject. He wanted to take the most American of all subjects — and make it his."[1]

Charles Lindbergh crossed the Atlantic in his Ryan NYP high-wing monoplane on 20 May, 1927. After 33½ hours of non-stop flying, he reached Le Bourget Aerodrome, having connected Paris to New York by air for the first time. A crowd of 200,000 pushed aside two companies of troops as they surged to greet him. "Lucky Lindy's" exploit fuelled public interest in civil aviation, and he became one of the most respected Americans of his time.

The year of Warner Bros.' film, 1957, marked the 30th anniversary of Lindbergh's flight. As bold red credits and a prologue appear on screen, Franz Waxman's stirring theme (a passage of bargain basement Sibelius), announces the commemorative mission of this prestige film. In a decade of glowing color movies shot in widescreen formats, *The Spirit of St. Louis* looked set to cash in on a Hollywood infatuation with the '20s marked by such films as *Singin' in the Rain* and Wilder's own

Some Like It Hot. Indeed, the recent British video of the film touts all the excesses of the "Roaring Twenties" by way of a blurb. That the film was one of the biggest commercial failures with which Wilder was ever associated may be due to Lindbergh's questionable wartime politics, his lack of appeal in an age of hourly European departures from American cities, or the burgeoning public interest in space travel. As co-screenwriter Wendell Mayes commented: "I think they should have called it *The Lindbergh Story* or something like that because when they put it out as *The Spirit of St. Louis* everyone seemed to think it was an old musical...."[2] Mayes' comment is ironic since *Meet Me in St. Louis* is one of Hollywood's most enduring slices of Americana. Arguably, so is *The Spirit of St. Louis*, a film which has been read as a failed exploit and an anomaly in Wilder's oeuvre. I would like to argue for it as an inspiring and enjoyable film, and one which is central to Wilder's vision.

Wilder was alerted to Mayes' suitability for this project when he read a review in the *Los Angeles Times* of a TV play Mayes had written, set among the members of a Midwestern American family. Wilder persuaded his producer Leland Hayward to hire Mayes. The result is characterized not, as is the archetypal Wilder screenplay, by witty and delectable prose, but by richly authentic history. Leavened with comical homespun flashbacks, the screenplay is an adaptation from the aviator's own memoir detailing his resolve to undertake the flight, the building of the plane, and the flight itself.

The project does seem an unlikely one for Wilder. The impression it gives is of a European sophisticate wanting to reiterate his "American" credentials by making an action movie. It is a project which begs for a Raoul Walsh or a John Frankenheimer. You sense that Lindbergh's exploit is too conventionally heroic, too unambiguous, for a director who excels in the foibles of human nature. When Wilder met Lindbergh, his impression was of a man who "had become a Scandinavian Viking hero, without flesh and blood."[3] He found him "stand-offish" and "not easy to get through to."[4]

Brought up on a Minnesotan farm of Swedish stock, Lindbergh said little, preferring to tinker with the Model T in the yard and run the family holding. He was an American pragmatist, with none of the complications of the Easterner or European. His autobiography is the work of a man who came to pondering late in life. Although impressed by his exploit, for Wilder "he was an aristocrat by nature ... I never dared to make a wisecrack in his presence and I was embarrassed to ask him about his personal life."[5] In a screenplay trading largely in the pragmatics of the flight, Wilder was tempted to dramatize an anecdote in which a reporter paid a waitress to sneak up to the "Lone Eagle's" Garden City hotel room on the night before his flight so that he could lose his virginity, offering Wilder eloquent motivation for Lindbergh's sleepless night.

Reviewer Henry Hart in 1957 was disappointed that the screenwriters had overlooked the philosophical content of Lindbergh's account. But what interests Wilder and Mayes are the intricate arrangements in a grand plan, as well as the celebration of an American pioneer. Wilder is interested in how Lindbergh did it. Indeed, his film could be regarded not only as the fictional representation of Lindbergh's exploit, but a metaphor for Wilder's exploit of filming it. Like Lindbergh, Wilder had an aircraft especially built. He then shot the film along the route which Lindbergh took; the Great Circle Flight Line out of New York to Boston, to Newfoundland and Nova Scotia, across southern Ireland, Cornwall, and finally down the Seine. It is as though Wilder performed the feat again, this time for the cameras. In common with numerous Wilderian scams, his hero's scheme is meticulously thought through. He knows precisely where he is going, and won't even take a radio because it will unbalance the aircraft. He will navigate by the stars. He is a young man with a mission. Lindbergh's resolve lends *The Spirit of St. Louis* a self-fulfilling trajectory which is reminiscent of such as *Double Indemnity* and *Ace in the Hole*.

As Hart explains, "The pre-flight Lindbergh is portrayed as a shrewd bumpkin instead of as one of the initiated, i.e. one of that elect company of human beings who have volitionally risked death for a purpose."[6] Aside from ominously evoking the elitist Lindbergh of conciliatory trips to Nazi Germany, in his enthusiasm for the Viking hero, Hart fails to appreciate the appeal of the "booboisie"[7] bumpkin for Wilder, Mayes, and a Hollywood sold more on heroic firsts than rhetoric.[8] When interrogated by the conductors on her flight across the Midwest, Sue-Sue Applegate tells them that she is of "Swedish stock." As he demonstrated in *Hold Back the Dawn*, there is a Wilder who wants to commemorate the American melting pot, that cultural cauldron from which he and his audiences have emerged. And in *The Spirit of St. Louis* he relished the opportunity to indulge in a kind of visual vulgate. Such flashbacks as find Lindbergh setting his rickety plane down on a spick-and-span Army airfield, its inner tubes bursting in cartoonish fashion, and in which he bandies words with a suspender salesman, evoke the American silent comedy and foretell the coarse humor of *Some Like It Hot* and *Kiss Me, Stupid*.

Ditching the philosophical musings does not mean that the flight itself doesn't approach the sublime. In contrast with the documentary mood on the ground, Lindbergh's isolation amidst often magnificent scenery makes, at times, for an almost mystical reverie. As Lindbergh, James Stewart's drawl actually adds to the soporific effect. As he lies awake on the night before the flight in a room bathed in the shadows of pelting rain, the scene is not unlike that dark night of the soul through which Don Birnam must pass in his hospital bed at Bellevue. Meanwhile, downstairs the clack of typewriters inscribes, and re-inscribes, the legend of the "Lone Eagle," just as Lindbergh once constructed his plane. The lobby looks just like the City Room in *The Front Page*, the camera meandering amongst the copy and providing a constant flow of background information to ground the drama. As the journalists record, and embellish, the facts, a scratchy recording of *Rio Rita*, a popular song of the day, issues through the wall into Lindbergh's room. It is an unexceptional realistic footnote in a rare and exceptional life. This is where Wilder's tribute lives: somewhere between a newspaper headline, an act of faith, and the brute facticity of a plunging altimeter.

If, for Wilder, Lindbergh was a "dry, factual man,"[9] his reminiscences make for an invigorating rehearsal of the American 1920s as an era of visionary capitalists and crazy dreamers barnstorming their way into history. Vexed by the need to flesh out what is a single-handed story, and keen to locate the drama in a folksy context, the screenwriters created *tableaux vivants* painted in flamboyant colors by Robert Burks and J. Peverall Marley. Red, white and blue balloons descending from the sky, skywriting biplanes spewing tricolored smoke leave us in no doubt about the film's patriotic agenda. An idyll near a well which "pumps sweet water from a Kansas prairie," accompanied by Franz Waxman's lyrical take on American folk idiom, is pure Henry King. When Lindbergh crashes on the Peoria-to-Chicago mail run, he meets O. W. Schultz, salesman for the "Atlas Suspender Company." In a good-natured exchange, Schultz denigrates "aeroplanes," flyers being "plain bughouse" for thinking they have a future. We "hold up the pants of the Middle-West," a pragmatic mission recalling Lindbergh's own pragmatism, if departing from its cosmopolitan aim. In the diner from which Lindbergh calls New York long distance to order a plane for the flight, he also orders breakfast: "couple of eggs over and hold the grease gun." The physical and cultural dichotomy between the down-to-earth Midwest and the sophisticated East and Europe partly derives its resonance from Wilder's own experience as a Hollywood pragmatist making films for the rest of America and the world. Such resonance invests *The Spirit of St. Louis* with a cultural significance rarely found in the work of American action directors like Walsh or Frankenheimer. If Wilder spent the '30s writing screenplays offering a notion of Europe as a world of decadence and moral bankruptcy, his take on Lindbergh represents the unequivocal high tide of a celebration of American vitality and modernity. Seen in this light, *The Spirit of St. Louis* increasingly resembles a Wilderian dream-scheme bathed in the vibrant hues of a Jazz Age sensibility.

After the company has announced itself in terms which would satisfy Henry Ford, at the Ryan factory in San Diego (not a million miles from the "dream factory"), Lindbergh finds foreman Mr. Mahoney frying fish. It is the occasion for another slice of Americana. Committed to trying out the "sand-dabs" first, Lindbergh then involves himself in the production of *The Spirit of St. Louis*. A montage of draughting, planing, stitching, welding, buffing and doping culminates in a serene test flight over Dutch Flats. Delineated here is an aesthetic of the practical in which creative endeavor is portrayed not as some muse-inspired mystery, but as a matter of specialist know-how, common sense, and a little hope. An often underestimated aspect of watching movies is the amount of information we derive about the world about us. This is frequently true in the case of classical Hollywood in which realistically motivated settings and cause-and-effect were the norm. *The Spirit of St. Louis* is unusually scrupulous in affording a factual account of aircraft design, flying procedure and geography, as each leg of Lindbergh's progress is charted. If there is a strong feel on Dutch Flats for the miracle of powered flight, placing Lindbergh in a direct line of ascent from Lilienthal and the Wright Brothers, this is a rationalist's miracle. Before he sets off across the Atlantic, an inventory of articles required on the flight is taken. As the mechanic checks down the list — "...ammonia ampules, flashlight, hacksaw blades, air pump, rubber raft..." — we sense a Wilder keen to count the cost in efficiency and know-how.

If until the end of the flight, Lindbergh rejects God as his guide in favor of an instrument panel and a pressure gauge, *The Spirit of St. Louis* nevertheless carries its own load of metaphysical baggage. Before he flies, the pilot lingers outside the hangar as though in brief communion with the dawn. When a small mirror is required to enable him to read his magnetic compass, a young woman in the crowd offers her make-up mirror, asking if she can sit in the cockpit. Lindbergh explains what the gauges on the instrument panel are for and asks how far she has come to stand in the rain waiting. "Philadelphia," she replies, because, after all, he needed the mirror. As Hart expresses it, "everywhere, in the most obscure lives, the young man about to risk his life had quickened goodwill, awe and love."[10] As the "Spirit" is taxied out to the muddy runway, the procession of head lamp beams resembles the torches of some murky pilgrimage. Here is reiterated the Enlightenment dream of Man's rational, technological triumph over the world around him. It is a triumph which is reflected in Hollywood craftsman Wilder's logistical triumph of filming it.

Lindbergh's take-off is spellbinding. Like the aircraft, the editing is superbly designed. Editor Arthur Schmidt juggles shots of the runway, the plane, Lindbergh's goggled concentration, the muddying undercarriage, Mahoney, the girl, back to the plane, … for as long as it takes Lindbergh to clear the telegraph wires and trees. Notice that the shots of the pilot find him visibly connected to the controls. Man and machine have never been more at one. It is an alarming passage, expressing just how many are being "carried" by that flimsy little aircraft.

Uncharacteristically for a Wilder film, the photography is a major production value. While Burks and Marley took care of air fairs over the flatlands, Thomas Tutwiler's aerial photography was considered a coup. A Canadian Air Force helicopter and a B-25 Mitchell bomber were mounted with cameras, pilot Paul Mantz having to be grounded constantly to take fresh direction from Wilder. The technical details associated with this long, complex, and expensive shooting schedule are something which Wilder has rarely been induced to discuss. An economist as a rule, he shot 200,000 feet of film which had to be pared down to 12,000. It is the only film for which he shot such a surplus, and in 1969 he confessed to leaving the ending to a second unit. The shooting is the subject of a very informative article in *American Cinematographer*.[11] Shot in CinemaScope, and in tones reminiscent of post-war issues of *National Geographic*, such moments as that in which Lindbergh drops down out of fog and cruises across St. John's Bay, and later, as the coast of Kerry County becomes imprinted with the shadow of the speeding plane, are some of the most cheering in all Wilder. Anyone who has ever been on an arduous and important journey knows how Lindbergh feels as he comes to realize that he has reached Dingle Bay, Waxman's jig ringing in their ears.

The descent into Paris is technically and symbolically brilliant, the city having allowed Tutwiler carte blanche to shoot at dusk just as it becomes its most radiant. In the context of Wilder's exportation of American ideas and idioms, the whizzing floodlights of "Lindy's" descent plot a spectacular moment in this trading pattern. Yet the Paris over which Lindbergh flies is the old pre-war Paris of the great boulevards, the Arc de Triomphe, the Seine, the romantic Paris of Hollywood myth. This is the city which Wilder essayed in pre-war screenplays, and returned to in 1957 for *Love in the Afternoon*. But more importantly, for Wilder and Lindbergh, the city is a concentrated statement of the cultural reach of a certain way of doing things.

If *The Spirit of St. Louis* is a "star production from the movie making machine,"[12] James Stewart propels it and towers over it. One suspects it is Stewart, not Lindbergh, who is the true portrait of Wilder's film. In this tribute to American heroism, the American hero is Stewart. A frequent returnee to TV screens, *The Spirit of St. Louis* owes its popularity largely to this likeable star's presence. Like Lindbergh, Stewart's image is that of the doer, not the thinker. And like Lindbergh, Stewart had, during World War II, been a flyer. Unlike Lindbergh, Stewart had a natural accessibility. Like Wilder, he found Lindbergh himself difficult to get to know. Studying the newsreels and Lindbergh's writings ("It didn't give me any help"), Stewart, on meeting Lindbergh, "suddenly realized I had no questions to ask him."[13]

The film's dependence on Stewart, the intensity to which we are exposed to the actor in a cramped cockpit in a film with no other stars, is reflected in the essential place which *The Spirit of St. Louis* occupies in Stewart's oeuvre. As the actor recognized when pushing for it, the role lends itself to a classic Stewart interpretation, having much in common with the definitive roles of the '30s.[14] Although much better, the film is in the same patriotic vein as the flying epic *Strategic Air Command*, a Stewart film from 1955 with aerial sequences shot by Tutwiler. As Eyles writes: "He is more human than in the westerns, prey to fatigue and boredom, pushing himself to the limits of endurance, while retaining that old determination to succeed in a quest."[15] Stewart draws upon all the resources of his screen persona: his boyishness, resolve, magnanimity, elation, even a hint of psychosis. Seen in film-historical terms, the young Philadephian could be regarded not simply as a Lindbergh fan and an interesting plot device, but as an anonymous representative of Jimmy Stewart's fan base. It is perhaps a revealing mark of Lindbergh's taciturnity that his only recorded response to *The Spirit of St. Louis* was to congratulate Stewart for remembering to tap the fuel gauge before contact as any good pilot would have done.

The Spirit of St. Louis ends with a frenetic ticker-tape parade shot on the occasion of the real Lindbergh's return to New York. Like the

Charles Lindbergh, American pragmatist. Lindbergh (James Stewart) links New York with Paris while Stewart links his name with Lindbergh 3 in *The Spirit of St. Louis.*

film's rigorous attention to detail, it is a measure of its status as a heritage movie about the '20s, like the '50s, an era of American triumphalism. As Sinyard and Turner write, if *Double Indemnity, Ace in the Hole, The Apartment* and *Kiss Me, Stupid* are variously virulent hate-letters to America, *The Spirit of St. Louis* is perhaps the nearest Wilder has ever come to writing a love-letter to the country of his adoption."[16]

10

Some Like It Hot

Released in 1959, *Some Like It Hot* is pivotal. Following the starch of *The Spirit of St. Louis* and the pastry of *Love in the Afternoon*, it inaugurated a series of any works which saw Wilder move from satire to burlesque. Set in the America of 1929, its parody of the period is not only in keeping with Wilder's interest in Hollywood heritage but elaborates upon a preoccupation with the American 1920s which inflects *Sunset Blvd.* and is indulged in *The Spirit of St. Louis* and *The Front Page*. *Some Like It Hot* is also one of Wilder's funniest and most vital works, and remains one of the richest and most popular Hollywood films of the post-war period.

Opening sedately as a hearse rolls along what Bernard Dick compares with Warner Bros.' stock *New York Street*,[1] *Some Like It Hot* sketches a freewheeling world of hoods in shiny Packards, bathtub gin, and jazz syncopation which owes more than a little to George Grosz. In *Some Like It Hot* the native humor and barnstorming display of Lindbergh's recollections have survived the respectful suffocation of Wilder's factual account. What he delineates here is the boom-and-bust sensibility of an era in which unemployed musicians must don women's clothing or die. Sinyard and Turner sum up the tone of Wilder's mission: "It is the period between Prohibition and the Depression, a part of the American past with an audacity and a style to which Wilder affectionately responds ... 1929 was, after all, the year of Wilder's entry into the film industry."[2]

While *Some Like It Hot* presages the farcical antics of such Wilder comedies as *One, Two, Three* and *Kiss Me, Stupid*, it also seems to draw the line beneath those Hollywood excursions into the '20s which had been fashionable during the '50s. Aside from Wilder's own films, there were *Singin' in the Rain* (1952) and *The Sun Also Rises* (1957). Allied Artists, from which Wilder's current employer, the independent Mirisch Corporation,[3] had emerged, produced the fine gangster movie *Al Capone* in 1959. But more significantly, *Some Like It Hot* celebrates the pleasures specific to the Hollywood star system more emphatically than perhaps any other Wilder film. Coming at the 30th anniversary of Wilder's entry into filmmaking, the film is a tribute to Hollywood's intramural practices. In its cast appear George Raft as the preening mob boss "Spats" Columbo, and Pat O'Brien as Mulligan, a cop derived from an assortment of turns as cops and priests at Warners in the '30s. Such staple henchmen from the undergrowth of '40s and '50s film noir Mike Mazurki, Harry Wilson and Nehemiah Persoff can also be found lurking in the bit parts. Joe E. Brown as the lecherous millionaire Osgood Fielding III seems to have been designed by nature to exclaim "Zowie!" at key moments for Wilder and Diamond. One of the film's key elements is an impersonation by the Tony Curtis character Joe/Josephine of the Cary Grant of the pre-war period. Raft, O'Brien, Mazurki, Wilson, Brown, Curtis, Monroe: *Some Like It Hot* is a summary of all that these actors ever were in movies. Only Jack Lemmon emerged to be something more.

Stepping woodenly through the film as he passed through many another is Raft. Although he continued to act into the '80s, *Some Like It Hot* feels like the swan song of his career as the quintessential urbane screen gangster. For David Thomson, here is the "saddest and most scathing picture of Raft ... where, as the starch-faced "Spats" Columbo, he has to watch his own coin-tossing tricks being paraded before him and then suffer an assassin jumping out of a premature birthday cake."[4] Raft is even obliged to emulate his old rival James Cagney by threatening an associate with a grapefruit in the face in a direct steal from *The Public Enemy* (1931). Raft's last line — "Big joke" — not only underlines the audacity of Columbo's assassin but underlines Wilder's audacious assassination of Raft's image. But as McBride and Wilmington observe, "Sometimes the worm turns — Edward G. Robinson, Jr. flips a coin a la George Raft in 'Scarface' and Raft, angered, snatches away the coin."[5]

In Tony Curtis' impersonation of Cary Grant, he and Wilder achieve the interesting assignment of evoking a slice of Hollywood's heritage and parodying a slice of its present. Corliss' assertion that it offered Curtis the long-nurtured opportunity to play Grant is interesting and

perceptive. Curtis feeds such residues of *His Girl Friday*'s[6] Walter Burns
as he found in Joe into a skit on the practiced man-about-town of recent
films like *An Affair to Remember* (1957), rendering Grant a pebble-spec-
tacled impotent. For Corliss, Curtis-as-Joe-as-Josephine-as-early-Grant
metamorphoses under Monroe's abundant caresses into Curtis-as-Joe-
as-Josephine-as-late-Grant before our very eyes. Curtis' coup becomes
the more telling when we recall that Grant's unworldly advertising man
also grows up fast in 1959's *North by Northwest*. In a film which evokes
the frenetic sight gags of the silent movie and the frenetic chatter of the
early talkies, Wilder "tells how Monroe helped Curtis shrug off the
accouterments of an early-talkie acting style and how Joe E. Brown

Jerry and Joe, American transvestites. *Left to right,* Jerry as Daphne (Jack Lemmon) meets Joe/sephine-as-early-Cary-Grant (Tony Curtis) in *Some Like It Hot,*
Mirisch Corporation, 1959. *Right,* Sugar Kane Kowalcik smooths the path.

trapped Lemmon into the awful transsexual consequences of an effeminate movie presence."[7]

It is a transformation which seems to highlight a fundamental feature of Wilder's working philosophy. By deploying and reviewing the clichés of the past, Wilder offers a case study in Hollywood survival. Reflected here is the boom-and-bust nature of Hollywood, a town in which you're only as good as your last credit. Wilder knows that, in searching for a winning formula, you have to use anything that works. Otherwise, you become as obsolete as the clichés themselves. As Lemmon, a key component of '60s Wilder, said: "Actually, *Some Like It Hot* is one long series of clichés, older than putting a lampshade on your head and pretending you're a guy dressed as a dame."[8] But if *Some Like It Hot* is about the American 1920s and pre-war Hollywood, it is equally Wilder and Diamond's attempt to inaugurate the '60s with a film which heralds both the stylistic wackiness of that decade's comedies and the sexual fluidity of its mores.

Sinyard and Turner's account of polarities in flux sensitively describes some of the dynamics which power the comedy. The spiritual journey from the deathly night-world of Chicago streets, garages, and funeral parlors to the palms, verandahs and gilded hotels of Miami is crisply evoked. But the comparison they make between Miami and such rejuvenating European resorts as *Ninotchka*'s Paris and *Avanti*'s Ischia can only be taken so far. The atmosphere and values of Paris and Ischia may provide dramatic contrast, but Miami's are the flipside of the same crazy era as Chicago's. Wilder's Miami is as florid, crass and potentially fatal a venue of '20s excess as the arch location of '20s gangsterism. Very temporary respite it may be, but the jazz is just as feverish, while the booze is as sought after as anywhere in America.[9] The rubbing-out of "Spats" is just as brutal as the rubbing-out of "Toothpick" Charlie which led to Joe and Jerry's fleeing Chicago.

The writers argue that Chicago is predominantly a male world, while Miami is predominantly a female one. But Miami is not by comparison with that train on which the only apparent male is the diminutive and put-upon band manager Beinstock. In this all-girl preserve, the "girls" are treated to a berth packed with Sugar (Monroe) and a bevy of beautiful girls, and must contend with dormitory confidences and "chests," real or imagined. Meanwhile, in spite of band leader Sweet Sue's prohibitions, Miami yields shriveled, sex-starved millionaires as predatory as the Chicago hoods. There is a bellboy who pursues Daphne and Jerry with slick and confident zeal. If the girls take the "girls" to their hearts without question, Josephine and Daphne are pursued as ardently by men in Miami as Joe and Jerry are in Chicago. With its plush hotels and abundant opportunity for role-play, Miami could also be seen as a metaphor for Hollywood itself, a community of hopeful starlets, ravenous agents, and other species of shark.[10]

Miami's holiday atmosphere provides the setting for Joe and Jerry's reappraisal of their sexual identities, as well as breaking Hollywood taboo by rendering their disguises convincing. In 1958 Wilder became involved in the second of his most productive professional "marriages" by choosing I. A. L. Diamond to co-write *Some Like It Hot*. In Zolotow's words: "He was a quiet, soft-spoken, scholarly person, nondescript in appearance, almost invisible on a set ... as intensely devoted to the art of film as Wilder, as knowledgeable about it as Wilder."[11] A seasoned screenwriter, Diamond "knew how to fit the pipes together,"[12] and the writers collaborated on all of Wilder's remaining films. Between them they came up with the St. Valentine's Day Massacre as the device which would lend credence to Joe and Jerry's continuing masquerade. Diamond remembers: "We set certain ground rules. One was that nobody was going to shave or smoke a cigar. The second thing we decided was it had to be a matter of life and death.... They had to be trapped."[13] Having witnessed the deaths of "Toothpick" Charlie and his men in that infamous garage on Clark Street, the boys go on the run, but are subsequently unable to reveal their identities to the women in the band. Yet their transvestitism is instructive for aiding the manifestation of their hidden selves. These superficial transitions from male to female have the effect of reconfiguring the men's characters, changing Joe from predatory to understanding and Jerry from suppliant and confused to exuberant and confused. As so often for Wilder's penniless, creative protagonists, the scheme which they embark upon to survive leads to self-knowledge and an enriched outlook. They change just as Wilder has. And while reinvention has enabled Wilder to grow and learn his craft, it enables these boys to become men by making them live as women. Gerald Mast shows that their transitions also prove instructive for Hollywood. "Wilder's game with sexual stereotypes also burlesques the way Hollywood conventions reduce people to bodies.... Wilder uses female impersonation to comment on the inhuman stereotyping of roles. As men, Tony Curtis and Jack Lemmon are distinct sexual types — the one sexy, suave, virile ... the other weak, passive, helpless.... But when they dress as women, they switch personalities. Joe becomes Josephine — soft, seductive, demure, genteel, refined, the kind who "gets" her man. Jerry becomes

Daphne — spunky, vivacious, full of life and pep, the kind who laughs then cries at parties. Tony Curtis, both as male and female, plays the sexual cliché; Jack Lemmon, both as male and female, plays the sexual departure — too passive as male, too aggressive as female."[14]

When Joe makes a phone call to secure the Florida dates, he adopts a falsetto. Considered daring at the time, for Peter John Dyer in *Sight and Sound*, Curtis was "a shade too real for comfort."[15] It seems ironic (and perhaps revealing) that "Curtis was shyer about getting into women's clothes than Jack Lemmon, who is an all-out clown and an extrovert."[16] Watching Curtis as the feminized and attractive Josephine, it comes to make sense that his first acting role which had any impact was as a little girl in a neighborhood adventure drama in the Bronx. From the phone call to the shot of Josephine and Daphne hurrying down the platform to join the rest of the girls, we witness one of Wilder's most consummate illusions. But Joe's easy assumption of femininity is matched by his altering perspective on male-female relations. When Sugar seduces her millionaire on Osgood's yacht, we witness a subversion of the standard Hollywood seduction which will culminate breathtakingly in Josephine's kissing Sugar at the end. Persuading Sugar that he is frigid following an accident in which he kissed the girl he loved and she fell into the Grand Canyon (Wilder's take on Hollywood's perennial "power of love" scenario), Sugar accepts the challenge, smothering the supine Joe in loving kisses so as to restore his smashed ego. The Lothario Joe then begins to realize that real lovemaking is not about taking but about giving. "Now you know how the other half lives," he tells Daphne as "she" emerges, outraged, from a lascivious encounter in the lift. In a conversation with producer David O. Selznick, Wilder had to convince him that tommy guns and Chicago rub-outs could be funny. In retrospect, Josephine's taking Sugar's tear-stained face in her hands and kissing her on the lips seems far more radical.

This is the moment when Joe proves that, by "becoming" a woman, he has become a mensch. It is one of the tenderest resolutions in Wilder's entire corpus, deriving huge resonance from Monroe, for whom Hollywood had meant emotional hardship and confusion, not least during the making of *Some Like It Hot*. For Corliss, "It is a moment as bizarre and powerful as anything in *Sunset Blvd.* ... For the gabby, grabby little men whose portraits Wilder so often drew, it marks a coming of age, almost a redemption. And those who think of Wilder as a small-time cynic, peddling imitation Berliner "Weltschmerz," will find their definitive refutation in the conviction, technique, assurance, and audacity of a simple kiss between an aging sex queen and a Bronx boy in drag."[17] All smarmy double-talk, we recall how Joe seduced Nellie Weinmeyer out of the keys to her Hupmobile in Chicago. By comparison, Sugar's kisses and Josephine's response are emphatic and unequivocal. In a film in which the men are either weak — Jerry, Osgood, Joe and his millionaire, 'Toothpick' Charlie — or wicked — "Spats" and his men — whilst the women are tough but exploited — Sugar, Sweet Sue — Joe's transformation constitutes the film's chief thrust. *Some Like It Hot* is a tribute to Curtis and a summation of all that he could have been. It is also a trailer for all that Lemmon is going to be.

If the burden of the conventional Hollywood closure falls to Joe, Jerry is in flux throughout. While the measure of Joe's sexual know-how is his ability to assume female garb and then leap back into male garb, but become a different male, Jerry dresses up as a female but remains unsynchronized, like a traced outline constantly departing from the thing traced. Notice how his hairy calves threaten to sabotage the scheme on the platform. Jerry must be told what he is — "You're a girl/I'm a girl," "You're a boy/I'm a boy"— by the chameleon Joe/sephine. In Lemmon's hands, Jerry remains Joe's stooge (as C. C. Baxter will become Sheldrake's in *The Apartment*), a dopey musician in drag without a note of subtlety. Yet the "dirty curve" which apparently prevents Jerry from adapting has given birth to a frumpy and faithful girlfriend to every girl Daphne meets. While the band recalls those unruly kids in *Hold Back the Dawn*, and the men are as randy as those cadets in *The Major and the Minor*, Daphne is the biggest "kid" in the film. Mirroring Jerry's helpless role vis-à-vis Joe, "she" offers the possibility of a fresh start for the Hollywood sexual stereotype, just as Susan Applegate derived fresh empowerment from her disguise.

Yet *Some Like It Hot* merely charts a new world; it doesn't venture to explore it. While running from every Wilder "taker" she ever fell for, Sugar has found in Daphne, according to convention, the biggest wisecracking friend a Hollywood heroine ever had. Jerry never escapes his female fate and so it seems appropriate that he should become the heroine's buddy since convention dictates that she should be funny but never a threat to her best friend, the bearer, with Joe, of the conventional closure. Claiming Sugar's gin flask to protect her from Sweet Sue's prohibitions, and looking like a mannish version of her buddies Sugar and Joe/sephine, Daphne/Jerry is heading into a sexual cul-de-sac which is finally sealed, as everything in Wilder is, by a line of dialogue. Following escalating protests to the smitten Osgood, the daffy Jerry finally confesses that "she" is a man. Osgood's famous reply—"Nobody's perfect"—briefly interrogates a world of pat Hollywood stereotypes and encapsulates the predicament of Lemmon from that point on. If he is not in thrall to his friend, Jerry is thrown onto the mercy of a cold and cruel world. It is a condition which Wilder will delineate in future Lemmon characterizations. It is also a condition, Ruth Wisse explains, the roots of which run deep in post-war Jewish-American fiction: "The schlemiel is the active disseminator of bad luck ... (His) misfortune is his character. It is not accidental, but essential.... The schlemiel's comedy is existential, deriving from his very nature in its confrontation with reality."[18]

Like the forthcoming *The Apartment*, *Some Like It Hot* is set, at least partly, in an urban world with a strong Jewish flavor. Aside from Curtis (originally Bernie Schwartz), it contains Billy Gray's piquant turn as theatrical agent Sig Poliakoff. While the good-hearted schlemiel C. C. Baxter will hold *The Apartment* together, Jerry will always take a downbeat view and run up against hitches in his dealings with the world. All his actions are determined by Joe, whatever the cost; to put their wages on a greyhound, to play a date 100 miles away on a freezing February night, to dress up as women and infiltrate an all-girl band in Florida. Jerry complains, but he never acts. He is acted upon. And while his friend ends up with the girl, Jerry must remain on the sidelines, ever the outsider. Or marry Osgood. But even when he entertains the idea of marrying the millionaire for his money after a night of tangoing till dawn (cruelly mocking Joe Gillis' New Year's date with Norma), he is dissuaded by Joe. Their celebrated exchange: "Why would a guy wanna marry a guy?" "Security" sums Jerry up in a word. At least with a guy he'll never be unsure again. Embodying reminders of those other compromised Wilderian schlemiels Joe Gillis and Richard Sherman, Jerry is at the mercy of every temptation and indignity which Wilder can heap upon him. Tagged by his first Hollywood studio, Columbia, in 1953 as "a guy you're gonna like,"[19] Lemmon had begun the rehearsal which over five subsequent Wilder screenplays would help define him as the well-meaning American male struggling to make sense of a world in which essential decency alone just won't do.

Some Like It Hot delineated the Monroe screen persona of injured innocence and blithe humor better than any other film until the authentic Marilyn is said to have emerged in Huston's *The Misfits*, written by third husband Arthur Miller in 1961. For Corliss, her rendition of "I'm Through with Love" is worth all the Method performances she never gave; it encapsulates a tawdry childhood, three disappointing marriages, the adulation/mockery of curious fans, even a final, abortive phone call."[20] Along with Roslyn Tabor, Sugar Kowalcik/Kane is the definitive role in the actor's career. And like Roslyn, Sugar perhaps expresses something of the Beat generation sensibility of the age. Out of control, running who knows where, Sugar practices Roslyn's bid for freedom from a world of "takers" and taken. Like the Girl who drives Richard Sherman to apoplexy in *The Seven Year Itch*, Sugar is blissfully unaware of the effect her sexuality has on the men around her. But unlike the Girl, she has gained maturity enough to realize that the world is far from perfect. The moment when Joe's millionaire leaves her, dropping some flowers and a bracelet given to Jerry outside her hotel room, is a quintessentially forlorn Wilder moment, in the same vein as Sheldrake's offering his mistress Fran Kubelik $100 before going back to spend Christmas with his family in *The Apartment*.

As the reviewer in the *Monthly Film Bulletin* realized in 1959,[21] Sugar is not as real as Monroe. Her protestations of emotional vulnerability reflect upon Monroe herself and remain central to the film's intramural mission. In an allusion to her famously dumb verdict on classical music in *The Seven Year Itch*, Sugar claims to appreciate it in order to impress Joe's millionaire. This Monroe variant is the Girl's gentler sister. Indeed, the seeds of Sugar's desire for the shy bespectacled type can be found in the earlier film, while *Some Like It Hot* suggests a full-blown reference to Monroe's marriage to Arthur Miller.

"Have you tried American women?" Sugar asks her frigid lover. As Sinyard and Turner observe, Wilder brought out a brash vulgarity and an "innocent sexiness"[22] in Monroe which fills the air with double entendres which, because they involve a play on words — "If it wasn't for you, I'd be in the middle of nowhere sitting on my ukulele" — remain funny and foiled the censor. It also seems entirely in keeping with Wilder's perception of the American style. In common with Joe, and Wilder protagonists like Sefton, the Girl and Lindbergh, there is a strong streak of pragmatism in Sugar. While Joe dons disguises at the drop of a hat, she organizes midnight feasts on the train, sings and plays the ukulele, and survives in spite of everything. Sugar Kowalcik and Fran Kubelik may be dumb romantics from the hinterland — Sugar hails from Sandusky, Ohio — but their native grace enables an optimism whatever the circumstances. A cynic may say that, dopey as she is, Sugar gets her millionaire with a life story at least as strategic as his.

Consonant with the film's broad farce, the characters are defined with broad brush strokes. And to complement this substantial sweep,

Wilder is keen to deploy his customary quota of loaded objects. On two occasions, "Spats" Columbo's entrance is metonymically announced by a shot of his trademark footwear; when Sugar strides along the platform in Chicago, turning heads, steam spurts from between the bogies of the train; later, her rendition of *Runnin' Wild* introduces a shot of the racing train wheels propelling the action; a coffin fronts for a case of booze; a hearse's upholstery for a stash of tommy guns; "Mozzarella's Funeral Parlor" becomes a speakeasy swinging to "Sweet Georgia Brown"; gas pours from a Hupmobile tank like blood from the bodies of dying gangsters; Sugar tells Joe of her past disappointments — "This is gonna be the biggest thing since the Graf Zeppelin" — while Dolores mocks Beinstock with a trombone raspberry; reflecting advances made and rebuffed behind closed doors. A swish pan shows the floor indicator on a hotel lift fluctuate in cartoonish fashion, then whips us from Joe and Sugar's moonlit tryst to Jerry's with Osgood and back again. Such extravagance of device and dialogue reflects the film's shifts from carnage to comedy and back again.

It is also matched by a broad approach to the visuals. By comparison with the somber streets of Chicago, Miami is one long splash of dazzling daylight and moonlit night. Only in Chicago do the streets glisten so blackly. Only in Miami (or California) do the beaches glare so vividly. Wilder shot the film in black-and-white partly because, until the late '60s, he still preferred monochrome, and partly because he felt that the clarity of color would militate against the playful illusion that Curtis and Lemmon's act would generate. It would also detract from the period allusions which Wilder and Diamond were trying to generate. Notice the play of light and shade along the corridors of that ornate Miami hotel. In this tribute to the crazy '20s, that overwrought pile recalls strange goings-on in Wilderian settings from Los Feliz Boulevard to Sunset Blvd.

11

The Apartment

It is instructive to see *The Apartment* as the most optimistic of three Wilder essays, all set in the world of insurance, which pit the solitary individual against the anomie of Big Business. If *Double Indemnity* in 1944 charted the ethical prospects given the post-war rise of the multinational corporation, *The Apartment* in 1960 was a call for redemption as the era of the Corporation Man reached its zenith, while *The Fortune Cookie* in 1966 reaffirmed the notion of the individual as architect of an individual destiny. What makes *The Apartment* the most uplifting of the three is that individual redemption is here most fully realized. While critical doubt persists over Phyllis Dietrichson's regeneration and Harry Hinkle's self-affirmation, C. C. "Bud" Baxter (Jack Lemmon) and Fran Kubelik (Shirley MacLaine) are temperamentally unable to reconcile themselves to a society which thrives on the buying and selling of human dignity.

As with a number of Wilder films, the end of *The Apartment* has been described as a bland concession to the box office. It is true that Fran's dash through midtown Manhattan, hair blowing in the wind, Adolph Deutsch's score surging behind her, feels like the Happy Ending of Hollywood cliché. But her reasons for returning to Bud's apartment feel as fated as Phyllis and Walter's self-destruction. Indeed, these screenplays may be the most well integrated in Wilder's canon.

Fran's decision to flee a difficult relationship with the married man Sheldrake (Fred MacMurray), which leaves her feeling suicidal, for someone who is not only available but at the same stage of self-discovery, seems thoroughly feasible. Resembling a *bildungsroman*, *The Apartment*

"Couldn't happen to a nicer guy." Frank Kubelik (Shirley MacLaine) shows C.C. Baxter (Jack Lemmon) her appreciation in *The Apartment*.

charts the emotional development of two young people who come to realize that the over-rational structures of their society are incompatible with devotion to an individual personality with all its quirks. Fran's asking Bud: "Why can't I ever fall in love with someone nice like you?"[1] signals the burgeoning recognition that devotion requires a nature capable of eliciting such devotion. But when she indulges in the fiction of her infatuation, her tone seems phony. "Maybe (Sheldrake) does love me — only he doesn't have the nerve to tell his wife"[2] contains romantic illusion, but also, paradoxically, an acknowledgment of Sheldrake's essential insincerity. The extent of Bud and Fran's compatibility can be summed up by the fact that her exploitation by Sheldrake saves Bud from collusion in Sheldrake's philandering, while Bud saves Fran's life. In this fairy tale, each comes to terms with his or her roles as, in Bernard Dick's words: "babes in the woods of big business."[3]

Fran has never acted, she reacts. She took the post of lift operator at "Consolidated Life" because she cannot spell and so failed the typing test. As a lowly lift operator, her self-esteem is so diminished that she attaches herself to a father figure. Fran's insecurity drives her to seek an identity as somebody's lover, and to find one as somebody's plaything. Stealthily balanced between comedy and tragedy, the saddest scenes in *The Apartment* find Bud and Fran caught in a completely rationalized world in which individuals are accounted in terms of what they have to sell and underwritten by the post-modern metaphysic of money rather than human kindness. When Fran characterizes this world as one of "takers" and those who "get took,"[4] she recalls the world of *Double Indemnity* in which a character is either scheming to beat the system or scheming to beat the schemer.

Daniel Mandell's editing reinforces Wilder's critique and even appears to reinstall a sense of continuity into lives reduced to moments of material and sexual gratification. For example, when a disconsolate Bud trudges away from the Christmas Eve office party, strip lights receding into the distance over his head, Mandell dissolves to a bar at which he drowns his sorrows, its counter receding towards the entrance on Columbus Avenue. Later, Mandell dissolves from the bar to the stairs leading Bud and barfly Margie MacDougall up to Bud's apartment. Later still, he cuts from a string of spaghetti tangled up in a tennis racket's strings used to strain it when Bud cooked for Fran, to a streamer looping over Fran's table at the New Year's Eve party to which Sheldrake has taken her.

Bud has done an evening class in Advanced Accounting. Arguably, office sexual politics is a branch of Advanced Accounting, one which emphasizes Bud's immersion in the universal rationalization of all human intercourse. The erosion of the individual by rational mechanisms is lent wry expression in Wilder's description of the interiors at "Consolidated": "Acres of gray steel desks, gray steel filing cabinets, and steel-gray faces under indirect light.... It is all very neat, antiseptic, impersonal. The only human touch is supplied by a bank of IBM machines, clacking away cheerfully in the background."[5] In this environment, the nature of a world which, under medievalism and under modernity, seemed to be guaranteed by the existence of God, is now brought to the individual's attention by the monotonous whir of computers. Notice how Bud's movements are governed by the machinations of his adding machine. Fran, meanwhile, does not so much control her lift as it controls her, along with the supervisor's clicker. Like her cab-driver brother-in-law, Fran ferries her social superiors to and fro. The Christmas present she gives Sheldrake is a recording of music from the Chinese restaurant where they meet and is entitled "Rickshaw Boy," an ironic comment about those who "carry" their betters, and are defined by the means of doing so. Bud's subsumption in this rationalized world is borne out by an enthusiastic introduction in which he relates that, were the entire population of New York to be laid end to end, the chain would stretch from Times Square to Karachi, Pakistan. Not only does the pointlessness of such information bear out the vacuousness of the system, but it graphically illustrates the laying low of humanity which Wilder criticizes. When Bud tells Fran of the average New Yorker's annual cold average, she sympathizes with those who, because she never catches cold, compensate with more than their share. Her attitude is symptomatic of her humanity. That everyone else subscribes to the self-service which such rationalization supports is illustrated by the "Consolidated" switchboard operators who, rather than cover for one another, scramble to get to the office party. That Bud is a conformist of the most pathetic hue is reinforced by his having a cold. And, like Polly in Wilder's *Kiss Me, Stupid* (who also develops a cold), he is aspiring under false pretenses to another lifestyle, along with many another Wilder protagonist. Prior to his moment of self-realization, he points out to Fran that it was not Sheldrake who was using him, but Bud who was using Sheldrake to get to the 27th Floor. It is only when he realizes that the whole climate of usury is corrupt that Bud becomes a "mensch — a human being."[6]

Bud and Fran's dilemma is such that, in aspiring to be part of the system, they depart from their better natures. Fran briefly gets Sheldrake, and Bud gets the top job. Yet this is not what they need in order to be self-respecting individuals. *The Apartment* is about people who, by pursuing the post-modern deities of Money and Status, have departed from their humanity, that which they have in kind with others. Fran's "Why do people have to love people, anyway?"[7] contains more than mere disappointment over a failed romance. It calls into question the very thrust of post-war American life. If the logic of commercial exchange attends Sheldrake's swapping tickets for *Music Man*[8] for Bud's apartment key; his promise to divorce his wife in return for Fran's love; and Margie's wanting to "buy"[9] Bud some music on the jukebox, Bud and Fran will become no less than an ethical Adam and Eve.

Wilder's setting the film around Christmas reinforces this theme. Traditionally, Christmas is a celebration of human solidarity. Yet the friendless "Buddy-Boy" sits in a bar on Christmas Eve, despondently arranging cocktail sticks in a circle recalling Don Birnam's "vicious circles" in *The Lost Weekend*. While Bud sits, disappointed after discovering that Sheldrake has been using his apartment to seduce Fran, Margie, to the strains of a Yuletide carol, tells of a husband who tried to beat the system in Wilderian fashion. The irony of a pair contemplating infidelity to *Adeste Fidelis* is pointed. The Christmas Eve office party remains a seminal dissection of that most insincere of traditions. In David Spiller's words: "couples necking in every chair, a line-up dancing on the tables, dancing in every chink of the screen, and the roar of a soundtrack mingling voices, music, and the chinking of glasses."[10] Amidst the bawdy revelry, Fran learns of Sheldrake's many infidelities from his secretary Miss Olsen, while Bud discovers the truth about Fran. This juxtaposition of revelry and disappointment is *The Apartment*'s keynote.

Yet the film interrogates the new amorality with the Old World morality of the Dreyfuss couple and the Kubelik family. Wilder is emphatic about the cultural and compositional dichotomy between the cold, hard automation at "Consolidated Life" and the antiquated but cozy turn-of-the-century brownstone house where Bud lives. Notice the quaint wooden fittings in the corridor outside Bud's door. Notice how Fran takes issue with the idiosyncratic, slovenly comforts behind that door.

Wilder's use of Yiddish inflections is never so much in evidence again until *The Front Page*, while *The Apartment*'s portrait of a decent man compromised roots the film in a cultural bedrock shared with such contemporary Jewish writers as Saul Bellow and Bernard Malamud. Bud is that Jewish staple, the lovable schlemiel, an innocent abroad who doesn't know how to play as rough as the game requires and ends up, like

Bellow's Tommy Wilhelm, badly in need of a friend. When they mistake him for a callous womanizer, Dr. and Mildred Dreyfuss, his neighbors, highlight the extent of Bud's departure from his better nature. Bud is a "fine boy"[11] whose behavior confuses his neighbors. And the more he drinks and carouses, the more confused they become. Like Don Birnam, Bud is at the center of his own vicious circle.

If the paternal Dreyfuss would like to kick Bud's "keester clear around the block,"[12] Sheldrake is Bud's wayward master. He is the bluff and duplicitous manager whom Walter Neff would have become if he had not met Phyllis Dietrichson. Even his name, Jeff, reminds you of "Neff." When Miss Olsen describes Sheldrake as a consummate salesman, the link with *Double Indemnity* is underlined. A smooth operator at "Consolidated," and a prim family man in White Plains, Sheldrake is everything that is vulgar and unimaginative about the post-war suburban managerial class. Notice how he constantly appeals to Bud and Fran to put themselves in his position. Such appeals would elicit sympathy except that Sheldrake never ever puts himself in anyone else's shoes. Sheldrake and *The Fortune Cookie*'s "Whiplash Willie" are "takers" and *The Apartment* is founded on the truism that relationships between "takers" and those they "take" are eventually untenable. When Fran quietly acknowledges Bud's regeneration, Sheldrake is perplexed. It is paradoxical, but perhaps a measure of their acumen, that Wilder and Diamond here acknowledge that words cannot always capture a moment of truth. Conversely, Sheldrake's imploring a distressed Fran back at the apartment — "Come on, Fran, don't be that way" — marks him as a cheat whose words take refuge in clichés.

While in his position as Sheldrake's assistant, Bud gives him the latest figures on women who leave "Consolidated" to get married. The moment is ironic because Fran will presumably eventually do just that. It is also symptomatic of Wilder's grip on theme and narrative. Sheldrake's ability to exist with one foot in and one foot out of office and home shows how far down the road of corporate corruption Neff might have traveled. Fran's imminent departure marks her as possessed of the same home-building sensibility as Dreyfuss and Fran's sister, married to cabdriver Karl Matuschka. But Bud's statement of this theme finds the roots of Wilder's plot buried deep in dialogue and mise-en-scène. In the scene in which Sheldrake tells Bud his marriage is over, Mandell cuts from profile close-up to profile close-up, emphasizing their confrontation over Fran. Yet, notice that when Bud and Fran leave work and he invites her to the show, they accompany one another in the same frame.

And when they meet in the lobby at "Consolidated," they face each other, both in the same frame. The film's final shot is a two-shot in which they sit alongside each other. Bud and Fran's compatibility is reiterated in dialogue and composition throughout the film.

In spite of their executive status, Messrs. Dobisch, Eichelberger, Vanderhof and Kirkeby are as preyed upon as the lowly Bud and Fran. When Dobisch goes up to the apartment with a Marilyn Monroe look-a-like, it is hard to tell who is exploiting whom. *The Apartment* elaborates upon the essaying of the male menopause which Wilder undertook in *The Seven Year Itch*. Fran even bitterly rehearses it to express her disappointment in one scene. Less of a locker room joke than the earlier film, *The Apartment* heralds the treatment of sexuality in all its grubbiness and pain undertaken in British and American films of the '60s.

Margie too is lonely. *The Apartment*'s sister film *Double Indemnity* is evoked as "Margie" is Neff's fictitious girlfriend whom Keyes suspects "drinks from the bottle."[13] When she is telling Bud about her husband languishing in a Havana jail, the pair seem more like projections of separate states of mind than individuals free to relate to others. She is as stuck in her isolation as he is in his disappointment. When the pair smooch to a slow blues, we are reminded of Joe's circuits of the dance floor with Norma Desmond on New Year's Eve. Hope Holiday's Margie may be her saddest cameo.

In *The Apartment*, mirrors do not so much conform to the filmic convention of revealing duplicity to the audience because we only ever see the character's reflection, never character and reflection at once. Rather, mirrors show characters who they really are. When Fran says that her broken compact "makes me look the way I feel,"[14] she not only reflects upon the injury which Sheldrake does her, but upon her role as "other woman." The fracturing of the waif-like suicide statistic from the self-respecting person whom Fran could be is revealed in Bud's shaving mirror, in which she sees the sleeping pills that she will take. Fran's mirror also forces Bud to see himself, his split reflection graphically revealing to him the split between pimp and dupe.

Another object which Wilder invests with significance is the key — that to the apartment and that to the executive washroom which comes with Bud's new position. A key is Bud's passport up to the 27th Floor, and the means by which he finds himself back at street level when he returns the washroom key when Sheldrake requests that to the apartment. The key is thus both symbol of Bud's misplaced pride, and his moral regeneration. That the object displaces the man can be felt when

Bud is locked out of the apartment, Dobisch having left the wrong key under the mat when he and "Marilyn Monroe" left.

Dick is perceptive in recognizing the significance which Wilder ascribes to each of the rooms in the apartment: "a suicide attempt in the bathroom, an abortive dinner in the living room, and a vigil in the bedroom."[15] Seen in this light, each room becomes a stage for a new conflict, actual or psychological, reflecting the atomized, combative society outside. Indeed, Wilder makes the most of his setting, and it gives its name to the film as though it were a character whose used and abused effects mirror the condition of its occupant. This is not lost on Wilder who wryly treats the lonely bachelor to a re-run of *Grand Hotel* on TV. Bud's alienation from traditional notions of a healthy American heritage is reinforced by his rejection of the westerns proffered by each channel he tries. Shooting on location, and identifying the apartment as part of "51 W. 67th," a brownstone "just half a block from Central Park,"[16] adds to the realism. That this house is not a home is further underlined by the fact that Bud only ever buys liquor to fuel his superiors' affairs and lives on TV dinners. Significantly, the only time he cooks a meal from scratch is when Fran is staying in the apartment. Like Sheldrake, Bud has one foot in and one foot out of his life. The extent of the post-modern American's sentimental departure from his or her fellows is voiced by Wilder: "We have a prefabricated loneliness in America.... With this loneliness goes the urge to better oneself and rise from the masses.... I portray Americans as beasts."[17] It is an issue with which Wilder's insurance triptych calls America to account.

Characteristically efficient in its look, *The Apartment* was shot on crisp black-and-white stock. The scene in which Bud, half asleep, slumps on a bench in Central Park, benches receding into the distance like those desks and lights at "Consolidated," while neons on Central Park South glint through the gloom, is all the more forlorn for being stretched across a Panavision frame. If we were closer to the neons, they might seem inviting. From here they just look lonely. As Bud sits, or lurks on an autumnal sidewalk waiting to use his apartment, we are reminded of those Edward Hopper canvases with their anonymous transients waiting in blocks of matt brown or blue. These are the kind of American urban tableaux which will drag Wilder devotees back to *The Apartment* again and again.

Gerald Mast writes of the flattened interior at "Consolidated" that the "geometric rows of desks, the regularity of the ceiling's fluorescent lighting, the clicking sound of business machines, the visual patterns that reduce people to mechanisms — has become a classic example of the use of composition for the wide screen."[18] Art Director Alexander Trauner had tiny desks and dwarves positioned in the middle distance, and tinier still positioned with cut-outs in the far distance. Sinyard and Turner write of a compositional structure which emphasizes the theme of social climbing through a series of oppositions between horizontal and vertical planes. Such a structure informs the opening shot in which the camera pans over Manhattan before tracking up the side of the "Consolidated Life" building. In the opening shot of the lobby at "Consolidated," Director of Photography Joseph LaShelle pans horizontally as humanity pours across to the lifts. That moving vertically inclines one to plummet ethnically here is hinted at in Fran's "Something happens to men in elevators. Must be the change of altitude."[19]

If Wilder has been a master of the star vehicle and *The Seven Year Itch* and *Some Like It Hot* were vehicles tailored to bring out the best in Marilyn Monroe, *The Apartment* and *The Fortune Cookie* are key Jack Lemmon vehicles. Lemmon's performance here is as rich in gesture and nuance as any the actor has given. Sinyard and Turner capture the historical importance of Bud Baxter. "It is a performance ... that Lemmon has been giving, off and on, ever since: his roles in subsequent Wilder films, and *Days of Wine and Roses*, *The Odd Couple*, *The Prisoner of Second Avenue*, *The Out-of-Towners* and *Save the Tiger* feed off Baxter's central tensions and owe much to the representation of contemporary America which Wilder established in *The Apartment*."[20] One could add *The China Syndrome*, *Missing* and *Glengarry Glen Ross* to the list. In an interview given to *Films and Filming* in 1960, Lemmon himself said: "The part that I had ... is far and away the best that I've had, and the part that has interested me most. The role combines comedy and drama and romance: and this is probably why I love the part so much, because it ran such a gamut."[21] If *Double Indemnity*'s tragedy is tempered by slick flippancy, *The Fortune Cookie*'s comedy underwritten by bitterness, the tragic and the comic meet in Bud Baxter. Every word and gesture of Lemmon's, however funny, bears a freight of melancholy. At one point, he gets in a crowded lift and rehearses a declaration of love which Sheldrake has already preempted by proposing to Fran. Later, pointing to a waiting brunette, he tells Fran that she is his date for the evening. When Fran leaves, we see the brunette met by another man while Bud strolls nonchalantly over to buy a paperback. The sad-funny truth is that Bud is an idiot who no self-respecting personnel director would want as his personal assistant. Lemmon plays Bud as an adorable worrier who continually struggles with his fate. Notice

Lemmon's consummate mime as Bud juggles his "clients'" appointments while coping with a runny nose. One of the actor's funniest moments occurs when, as Sheldrake warns Baxter of the consequences if his arrangements with Kirkeby and Co "leaked out,"[22] in his vehemence that it shouldn't, Baxter squirts nasal fluid over Sheldrake's desk. As biographer Michael Freedland writes, Lemmon is "Mr. Average or Mr. Everyman, and he is not ashamed of displaying characteristics of average men who, on average, like to keep those things quiet."[23] Lemmon's Bud is the culture's paradigm for fraught Urban Man. In the adding machine which dictates his movements, we can detect the "galopita-galopita machine" which will dominate the skyline from Stanley Ford's bachelor apartment in *How to Murder Your Wife* (1965). The episode in which Bud prepares spaghetti and meatballs anticipates the fastidious Felix in *The Odd Couple* (1967).

Shirley MacLaine gave one of her most winning performances for Wilder as the waif longing for a "friendly animal,"[24] in the urban jungle. MacLaine's rodent-like features contain just the right measure of wounded innocence to make Fran Kubelik appear disappointed but not embittered. As Dr. Dreyfuss struggles to keep her awake after her overdose, we are reminded of Lindbergh's fight to stay awake over the Atlantic in *The Spirit of St. Louis*, a journey as redemptive in its way as Fran's journey to self-awareness.

Jack Kruschen is perfect as Dreyfuss, dexterously orchestrating ammonia ampules, homespun wisdom and slaps to prevent Fran from passing into a coma. Another of Wilder's avuncular sages, Dreyfuss is one of his most keenly etched supports. Ray Walston as Dobisch is the slimy Orville Spooner of *Kiss Me, Stupid* given a little power. Naomi Stevens' gemütlich Mildred Dreyfuss remains one of few quintessentially Jewish figures in the Jew Wilder's oeuvre.

The Apartment arises out of its squalid details like a Zola novel, its funny moments casting welcome light into shadowy lives and lending perspective to a trend which, by implication, must spell social ruin. As Wilder has said: "Fluffy comedies about New York working girls who earn sixty dollars a week and live in all-white apartments and wear designer clothes will always be popular. But not with me. I want to go beyond the powder-puff school and find humor in a situation which is normally treated with solemnity."[25] The end of this fairy tale may for some still look like box-office compromise, but when Fran utters its closing line — "Shut up and deal!"[26] — we are reminded of Nora's predicament in Ibsen's *A Doll's House*. It is one thing to define oneself for oneself. But in dreams begin responsibilities.

12

Kiss Me, Stupid

In December, 1964 when *Kiss Me, Stupid* was released, cinemas across the South and Midwest suspended its run, and critics on both sides of the Atlantic described it as Wilder's most tasteless film since *Ace in the Hole* (with which it shares a striking affinity). *Kiss Me, Stupid* appeared in an era characterized by increasing social permissiveness and ever more ingenious ruses for exploring sex on screen. Enraged by its impotence in a changing world, the Moral Majority pilloried the film, the Catholic "Legion of Decency" giving it a "Condemned" rating. As Wilder wrote in early 1965 to the sympathetic Geoffrey Shurlock of the industry watchdog the Motion Picture Producers' Association: "It is obvious that the Legionnaires have been lying in the bushes, biding their time until they could waylay some picturemaker of import and use him as a whipping boy for the entire industry."[1] Shurlock's decision to support *Kiss Me, Stupid* probably precipitated the last important debate on censorship of sexual content in the history of Hollywood. What is at stake in censorship disputes are less importantly the sensibilities and reputations of self-proclaimed moral guardians and more crucially the aesthetics involved. Whilst we seldom remember the individuals, we usually remember the films. In this light, distributor United Artists' decision to hand responsibility for distribution over to Lopert Pictures, a subsidiary accustomed to handling foreign art films, reflects more tellingly upon Wilder's treatment of his theme than upon the theme itself.

Based upon an Italian farce, *Kiss Me, Stupid* is characterized most emphatically by the broad brush strokes of the genre. Of all the Wilder films of a difficult decade, it is probably the most difficult to like. Amidst the bawdy dialogue, the mechanical central conceit, and the ugly stock characters, there is none of the warmth of *The Apartment* or the sensibility which better players will bring to the forthcoming *The Fortune Cookie*. *Kiss Me, Stupid* foresaw much that was sexually frank in '60s Hollywood output, but now appears as one of Wilder's more indelicate attempts to set the trend.

Initially envisaged with Peter Sellers in the role of jealous husband Orville Spooner, Wilder had to reshoot with Ray Walston (the unlikeable Dobisch in *The Apartment*) when Sellers had a coronary six weeks into production. It is one of the tragedies of post-war film history that the excellent footage of Sellers is not available. Not only was he an actor with greater range and a sense of performance which encouraged audience rapport, but Sellers in retrospect seems to epitomize the little man's response to overbearing '60s sexual excess in a way in which the unsympathetic Walston could not. As critics noted, the coarsening of Wilder's work since *The Apartment* could be offset with stars like Lemmon and MacLaine. But in a film structured rigidly around stereotypes, we are confronted constantly with Walston and Cliff Osmond's charmlessness and their inability to react with the one-dimensional women whom they insult.

Kiss Me, Stupid is less morally outrageous than aesthetically crude. All structure, it leaves no room for reflection. The most memorable lines are clever rather than crafted. The title — "Kiss Me, Stupid" — epitomizes a trend in '60s Hollywood which, by pursuing the effect for its modernity, has left us with a label rather than a summation. Wilder's best films are either sustained by a powerful image — *Sunset Blvd.*, *The Apartment* — or a haunting phrase — *Five Graves to Cairo*, *The Fortune Cookie*. *Kiss Me, Stupid* now seems too clued-in to its time and does not roll off the tongue as other Wilder titles have.

What has also changed is our perception of what Wilder and Diamond were trying to do here. Ever since *Menschen am Sonntag*, Wilder has been interested in how ordinary people spend their leisure time. In the American films, this preoccupation has revolved around reworking the clichés and conventions of the movie business. Like many another Wilder film, *Kiss Me, Stupid* skillfully interrogates the audience expectations engendered by Hollywood. Sinyard and Turner are quick to see the title as a riposte to coy but aggressive Doris Day/Rock Hudson titles like *Pillow Talk* (1959) and *Move Over Darling* (1963). Shot in grimy blacks, whites and greys by Joseph LaShelle, drably furnished by Alexander Trauner, and set in an arid Nevada desert town, their reading of *Kiss Me, Stupid* as a blunt satire of the lush and affluent Day vehicles is persuasive.

But in this, Wilder's most anti–Hollywood Hollywood film, what hurts most is his cruelty. Positing the grotesque Walston as an ineffectual small-town failure in place of the usual flawed though likable Wilder hero, demolishing lounge lizard Dean Martin, and turning Kim Novak and Felicia Farr into blow-up dolls leaves no latitude for the exploration of the distance between representation and realism which gives point to satire. Also, one of the beauties of Wilder's films has been his and his actors' ability to make one sympathize with flawed characters. If he subverted Barbara Stanwyck's image in *Double Indemnity*, he and Stanwyck also gave Phyllis Dietrichson something which made us root for her. If he subverted Holden and Lemmon's images, between them they added something to complicate our resistance to self-seeking adventurers. Lacking the range and associations of Sellers, Walston has no way of tempering the grotesque extremes of Orville Spooner. As Wilder himself has said: "I got all I could from Walston."[2] By comparison, Dean Martin, an established screen presence, has a well-known self-mocking template to parody and enters into the conceit willingly and enjoyably. But Kim Novak as Polly the Pistol, a stock tart-with-a-heart, is unable to exceed the pneumatic limitations of the role. Stereotypes all, none of Wilder's actors are here able to import enough of the stuff of life into their roles to make us care whether they exceeded "Climax, Nevada" or rotted there.

Extending Wilder's examination of American popular culture, amateur songwriter Orville is an even more manic version of Wilder fantasist Richard Sherman in *The Seven Year Itch*. Whereas Sherman's fantasies are fueled by his position as processor of literary classic into pulp novelette, Orville's derive from a fatal cocktail of Beethoven and Tin Pan Alley. Orville and Barney are a pair of Wilderian schemer-buddies from the boondocks trying to break into the big time. Touting a little talent and a pedantic knowledge of song titles, Orville and Barney assault the American heartland and the aspirations of its citizenry so ferociously that one can, at least in part, understand the original damnation of the American critics. Orville and Barney are the doodle caricatures of an over-wise city slicker.

Based, like many Wilder scenarios, around its characters' deceptions, as critic Richard Lippe observed in the *Velvet Light Trap* in 1971, *Kiss Me, Stupid* is structured around the acting out of roles. This chimes with Wilder's interrogation of star images as well as being a key characteristic of the music industry to which Orville and Barney aspire. In order to protect his wife Zelda (Farr) against the lecherous transient entertainer Dino Martini, Orville must pretend that Polly, imported from the "Belly Button" roadhouse, is his wife. As Orville is stupid and has a jealous nature, it follows that Dino must be ejected from the marital home when he tries to do to Polly what she is usually paid to do. Orville's fantasy[3] thus forces Polly to play her cultural opposite, the adoring wife, a role she is willing to assume in awe of domestic bliss. Alienating Zelda so as to install Polly drives Zelda to the "Belly Button" to drown her sorrows, and thence to Polly's trailer where she, in awe of the singer, will masquerade as Polly and service the ejected Dino.

What this scenario enables is an unremitting satire at the expense of such Hollywood myths as that personal success equals sexual potency; that a female character can be either wife or whore, never both; and that marriage means happy ever after.

If anyone in the audience in 1964 still believed that personal success automatically makes one sexy, the spectre of the slavering Dino was meant to discredit the Hollywood playboy model for all time. Dino is "Dino," star of Vegas clubs and Hollywood TV specials. Slurring his wisecracks and suffixing every lascivious word with the ominous "Baby," Dino is the American rogue male run amok. At the heart of *Kiss Me, Stupid* is the withering deconstruction of Dean Martin. Handsome but useless, virile but thoughtless, Dino is the same when he drives out of Climax as he was when he drove in.[4]

Another myth satirized in *Kiss Me, Stupid* is that of the virtuous wife. When Orville and Zelda experiment with other partners, not only do they anticipate screen sexual freedoms to come, but they complicate Hollywood's model of womanhood by daring to suggest that a married woman can be virtuous or not, according to her mood.

In *Kiss Me, Stupid*, the impeccable institution of the Hollywood screen marriage is fraught with personal failure, insecurity and plain boredom. Orville and Zelda's is parody of this model. Whilst he is a gawky man-child, she is an American ideal: beautiful, intelligent and good. Theirs is one of the most dispiriting unions ever to have taken pride of place in a Hollywood film. Elsewhere is the scene in which Doro Merande and Howard McNear portray Zelda's Mom and Pop bickering on a Norman Rockwell porch. Wilder's assault on marriage as a staple Hollywood method of closure is unrelenting.

The scalding tone of Wilder's assault upon Hollywood mores leaves no room for the warmth which critics in the '70s began claiming for the film. Stuck with unrelenting remits, the characters never reflect upon their actions in a way which would lend them self-awareness. There is perhaps one moment of real poignancy. Joan Didion writing in *Vogue* delivered not only the most positive American critique of *Kiss Me, Stupid* to appear upon its release, but one of the most sensitive passages on Wilder ever. "What makes the picture so affecting, what makes people walk out when they will sit through and even applaud the real tasteless-ness, the true venality of pictures like *The Pink Panther* and *Bedtime Story*? They walk out, I suspect, because they sense that Wilder means it, that he would simply not be interested in pretending, say, that Clau-dia Cardinale could be a princess. The Wilder world is one seen at dawn through a hangover, a world of cheap double entendres and stale smoke, and drinks in which the ice has melted: the true country of despair."[5] What Didion puts her finger on here is that same despair which affects you in the shot of the hospital in which a man feigns paraplegia while another feels guilt over putting him there in *The Fortune Cookie. Some Like It Hot* has a similar dawn in which Joe and Sugar return from Osgood's yacht in which he has feigned millionaire status and she has become his lover, and pass Osgood returning from an assignation with Girl-Boy Jerry. The most affecting moment in *Kiss Me, Stupid* finds Dino driving away from "Zelda" while Orville drives Polly back as Zelda vacates her trailer. This dawn reversal is touching because it seems to catch the stereotypes off-duty, as it were, lending a glimpse at the humanity between the lines. Occurring between what Orville, Zelda and Polly became and what they could be, the scene seems to offer them a second chance. Cutting to a high angle establishing shot over the trailer, it also affords welcome respite from the claustrophobic to-and-fro of the plot. What Wilder realizes is that it is a characteristic of the end of wide-spread religious faith that men and women in a consumer society invest their hopes in schemes and binges which they believe may bring per-manent fulfillment but probably will bring only temporary solace. Such a realization informs Wilder's preoccupation with Hollywood as well as that of the moral guardians with Wilder.

Yet the moment is all too fleeting. Ultimately, *Kiss Me, Stupid* belongs to the uncultured pragmatist Barney. For him there is no truth beyond what can be seen, touched, heard, or smelled. If Orville is an artist with all the pathological symptoms but little of the talent, Barney is the fixer who makes the film happen around him, a mechanic who con-founds the passing big shot. Barney is a corpulent symbol of the spiri-tual waywardness of the film. Give him a copy of *Anna Karenina* and he

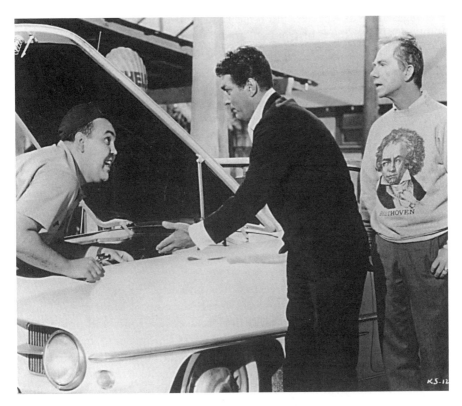

"I portray Americans as beasts." *Left to right,* Barney (Cliff Osmond) "fixes" Dino's car (Dean Martin) while Orville (Ray Walston) worries in *Kiss Me, Stupid.*

would use it to prop the door ajar if the air conditioning broke down. Whatever spiritual release is claimed on behalf of Polly and Orville is reduced by Barney to a rationale based upon record sales. He evokes what Wilder said of *The Apartment*: "I portray Americans as beasts."[6]

The broad humor of *Kiss Me, Stupid* is reflected in its broad visuals. The Panavision lens which evoked the elongated office and park benches in *The Apartment* here makes Dino's Italian convertible look like a stubby Metropolitan, and the chorus girls who flock around him at the Sands Hotel look like Watusis. Monochrome is perfect for the film since it enforces the poverty of lives lived in such a nowhere. Climax,[7] Nevada resembles the flyblown Escudero in *Ace in the Hole*. We never see the town as a whole, just Orville's place, the "Belly Button," and Polly's trailer. Climax is not a community but a series of sets in the desert. Axel Madsen sums it up: "Climax ... is a desolate place midway between Las

Vegas and Los Angeles, and it has road signs to dream cities: Salt Lake, Reno. It is a town of fronts of frame-bungalows where cocktail waitresses sleep in trailers surrounded by butane tanks, where time is told by television schedules, where no-one is beautiful or gifted; a town where petrol-station attendants dream of hitting the big time ... a place where the flesh is urgent because nothing else is."[8]

Perhaps the chief problem with *Kiss Me, Stupid* is Wilder's eventual inability to get us to believe for long enough in the human reality of his characters as effectively as he is able to get us to believe in the brute facticity of this dirty joke in the wilderness. The cinematography and the mise-en-scène convince us of the need for escape. The Venetian blinds in the Spooner house imprison Orville like his jealousy, an incongruous reminder of the psychological excesses of film noir which lends this drabbest of comedies an almost baroque edge. No more forlorn a symptom of cultural fracture exists than a Victorian love seat in the middle of Nevada.

Kiss Me, Stupid was released five days after the first major retrospective of Wilder's work opened at the Museum of Modern Art Film Library. Curator Richard Griffith's preface was ironic and poignant. "Wilder is the most precise, indeed relentless, chronicler of the post-war American scene, in shade as well as light, that the motion picture has produced."[9] *Kiss Me, Stupid* failed with most American critics (the Europeans have been kinder), because they could not see the satire and could not forgive Wilder for an acidic commentary without the sugar of known stars. The normally astute director had misjudged by pitching the film too far into the bleaker end of a formal continuum in which *The Apartment* had happily occupied the pivotal middle range. The American critical response was symptomatic of a decline in critical standing which began in 1960 and found Andrew Sarris consigning Wilder to the "Less Than Meets the Eye" slot in his 1968 auteurist bible *The American Cinema*. The trend was not to change until the critical establishment mellowed as Wilder's mellower late European works appeared. Meanwhile, *The Fortune Cookie* found him back on American soil and with friends.

13

The Fortune Cookie

At the beginning of the episode entitled "The Caper," Luther "Boom Boom" Jackson, the black football player responsible for putting Harry Hinkle into a wheelchair, is seen entering St. Mark's Hospital with a bouquet of flowers. It is a cold, grey Monday morning, and André Previn's bluesy dirge kicks in as the smokestacks of Cleveland belch in the distance. It is another of Wilder's melancholy "morning after" scenes. In this case the morning after lawyer "Whiplash Willie" Gingrich has announced his intention to sue on behalf of his brother-in-law. If Wilder's mornings after are the more melancholy for rubbing our noses in the reality of his fantastic schemes, this has to be one of the most God-forsaken Mondays in '60s American cinema.

The Fortune Cookie completed a classic Wilderian cycle of essays on American materialism, and inaugurated the double-act of Jack Lemmon and Walter Matthau. Less shrill than early '60s Wilder, *The Fortune Cookie* expands in formal style the exploration of the Great American Congame undertaken in *Kiss Me, Stupid*. Nervousness following that critical disaster perhaps lay behind United Artists' decision to re-title the film *Meet Whiplash Willie* for the British market, although this made little sense. *The Fortune Cookie* is one of Wilder and Diamond's best titles, encapsulating something of the snappy contrivance and vernacular sensibility which Wilder has made his own.

Wilder's Cleveland is a drab metropolis located partway between the New York of *The Apartment* and the Los Angeles of *Double Indemnity*. The third installment of what could be described as an insurance triptych, *The Fortune Cookie* unfolds a frenetic plan against the backdrop of a grimly realistic public life. This is a world in which materiality took precedence over humanity long ago. The insurance company from which Willie (Matthau) intends to collect — "Consolidated" — was the gaunt multinational which employed Bud Baxter. The very name suggests that an impulse to exploit has so consolidated itself that it runs in the national bloodstream.

Wilder and Diamond ironically reinforce the theme of the departure from traditional American values with nationalistic motifs. The message in the "fortune cookie" brought to Harry's bedside with a Chinese meal is Abraham Lincoln's: "You can't fool all the people all the time." Later, a TV commercial features a banal lyric touting linoleum to the strains of "When Johnny Comes Marching Home," while "Wave the Flag, Boys" is a running theme. Harry (Lemmon) and ex-wife Sandy (Judy West) were married on 4 July, but it is Harry's independence which becomes the issue. Boom Boom's Cadillac is the epitome of American class, while Harry's Mustang is a symbol of American virility (although for most of the film he is too incapacitated to use it). American football, of course, epitomizes the competitive impulse which the film satirizes.

The dichotomy between Good and Evil in this most structured of Wilder's films is painted in broad style. But the fable derives its resonance from a wider political context in which a white American and a black American can find solidarity in a society of grubby shades of grey. *The Fortune Cookie* was released in 1966, a time when race was an issue high on the American political agenda. It is another instance of the journalist in Wilder using the headlines as source material. But rather than place an African-American's search for self-determination at the center of this timely narrative, Wilder strapped Jack Lemmon into a corset and made him the instrument of a corrupt brother-in-law and the dupe of a trashy ex-wife. The principle remains the same. Meanwhile, star player Boom Boom (Ron Rich) is filled with guilt, is missing practice sessions and has begun to drink. What unites Harry and Boom Boom is the recognition in each that the other has been rendered only half a man.

A theme running through *The Fortune Cookie* is the importance of one's profession as a component of one's identity. Notice that the key characters are defined chiefly in terms of what they do. Although Willie has a wife and two children, he is a workaholic — "Where have I been? Working ... I've interviewed every person who was sitting between the twenty- and forty-yard lines — gotten signed statements from the groundspeakers — looked at miles of TV tape — instant replays — isolated camera."[1] Harry is a cameraman for CBS first seen following the line of

Harry Hinkle, American schlemiel. Playing upon the nature of Harry Hinkle's conscience, the British poster for *The Fortune Cookie* depends equally upon Wilder and the tried-and-tested Wilder/Diamond conceit. Yes, who is Harry Hinkle? … but also, what goes on here?

scrimmage from the sidelines at Cleveland Municipal Stadium. His affection for Boom Boom is clearly bound up in an interest in sport which he perennially covers. Purkey (Cliff Osmond), the surveillance expert hired by the lawyers to make sure Harry isn't faking, has the furtive nature of one for whom man and profession are one. Boom Boom is introduced as "a 220-pound Negro half-back."[2] 'The Legal Eagles' O'Brien, Thompson and Kincaid are introduced at home in opulent offices puffing on fat cigars. Only Sandy, defined mainly in terms of her sexuality, appears adrift, a wanna-be singer lacking the means to promote herself.

In keeping with this theme, the film's plot finds each character propelled by aims and ambitions which have the force of medieval humors. Willie wants to bring an insurance company down; Harry wants Sandy back; Purkey wants to bring Willie down; Boom Boom wants to assuage his guilt; Sandy wants a lot of money. But the morning after the scam has failed finds Harry out of money and probably out of a job, Boom Boom out of a job, and Sandy probably drifting back to New York. Only Purkey and Willie remain operational: Purkey by having tricked Harry into blowing his cover by maligning Boom Boom; Willie by rebounding with a case against O'Brien, Thompson and Kincaid even more compelling than the last.

The profession-as-identity theme has especial significance for Wilder. Disappointed by the poor reception of *Kiss Me, Stupid*, Wilder and Diamond needed a project which would reinstate them professionally. Although it was not, according to Maurice Zolotow, particularly successful with audiences or critics, the team was not as maligned as they had been in 1965. Plus, Walter Matthau, despite suffering a major heart attack during filming, gave one of the best performances of his career, winning the Best Supporting Actor prize at the Oscars. In retrospect, however, *The Fortune Cookie* is even better than this. If Willie sprightly comes back from failure, Wilder too came back with a formula which recalled his classic works and puts subsequent films in the shade.

The most persistent criticism of the film at the time was that Willie's scheme is so appealing — we all suspect insurance companies daily defraud the public — and its architect so compelling, that the redemptive ending in which, free at last, Harry returns to Boom Boom at the deserted Stadium, is a letdown. What left such a sour impression was that Good, when it eventually triumphed, seemed such an ineffectual affair. As Hollis Alpert wrote: "From *Sunset Blvd.* to *Some Like It Hot*, Wilder was imaginative, raucous, and had a way of running for touchdowns through a broken field of censors. This time around, he seems to have been tackled in advance."[3] But, as Stephen Farber realizes, Wilder's vision was too complex to give in to studio-imposed compromises. It is a letdown when the warm-hearted but dense Harry passes up the opportunity of $200,000. But there is a haunting ambivalence about that final scene. Wilder knows that we want to see the insurance company crooked and Harry get something for his pains. (He would never have formulated any of his plots if he hadn't recognized their potency.) Yet, in that gridiron romp, he sees an Eden-like innocence in which release is found in boyish camaraderie. This is the pitch where, as key Cleveland punt-returner and CBS cameraman, Boom Boom and Harry were at their best. Enshrining the uncomplicated gamesmanship and style which have always drawn Wilder to America, the scene speaks of a homespun wisdom from a time before the corporations defined the political and moral landscape. Dubbed a Virgo in the screenplay,[4] a virgin in a world of shysters and chisellers, little man Harry, with Boom Boom and like Bud and Fran, seeks a newer way to live. Harry is also here encouraging Boom Boom not to give up on his career and take the easy way out as Harry almost had. On that gridiron come together black and white and pre-war and post-war America. Indeed, the end of *The Fortune Cookie* is about the reconciliation of post-war America with itself.

Harry and Boom Boom were the latest in a long line of Wilderian buddies which stretches back to Walter and Barton Keyes in *Double Indemnity*. The character of Boom Boom has been described as an unconvincing caricature of the "good Negro." But, however uncomplicated he may be, this is not an unusual trait in a sportsman for whom, immured in the sporting profession, telling the truth and playing fair are traditionally central to the ethos. In addition, Boom Boom feels guilt about the accident which befell Harry, a fact often reiterated in the film and a key reason for Harry's turnaround. If anything, what Wilder and Diamond lacked when writing this character was a workable black version of the Jewish schlemiel, a character who, like Harry, is not simply kind but to whom the audience can feel superior.

It is significant that, despite Harry's insistence on blowing the chance of some big money, Willie is still fighting for his client at the bitter end. In film-historical terms, it is a portent of buddy relationships to come. As Jack Lemmon continued to extend the shadow of the good schlemiel across the '60s, Matthau's Willie is described in the screenplay as having "a brain full of razor blades and a heart full of chutzpah."[5] When this seedy figure in battered black tweed and felt hat first appears, smoking nervously, he dominates the plain white ward just as his scheme will dominate the film.

Farber realized that "Taking on a professional football team and the city of Cleveland and almost making his phony claim stick is a *creative* achievement of real substance."[6] It is perhaps the last of the great premeditated Wilderian schemes, with all the precision and artistry Walter Neff brought to crooking the house, Chuck Tatum brought to Escudero, and Sefton brought to *Stalag 17*. But for Neff and Tatum, feelings eventually won out over reason. Here, feelings are Harry's province. Reason is Willie's. And Wilder and Matthau's creation is a cartoon celebration of what happens when Reason, the key plank of an Enlightenment out of which America emerged, triumphs over feelings.

When Willie first appears, he filches the dime he has given his son to drop into a box for unwed mothers. Having used it to announce to the ironically-named *Cleveland Plain Dealer* his intention to sue, he tells Harry that they are in this "straight down the line."[7] Like Walter and Phyllis, they are bound to each other by their transgression. Just as Walter's 11 years in insurance seem to have been practically a preparation for their scheme, Willie has been awaiting such an opportunity as this to practice his. Only Wilder's mood has changed. If *Double Indemnity* was a pitiless nightmare, *The Fortune Cookie* is a "fine, dark, gag-filled hallucination peopled by dropouts from the Great Society."[8] What his reference to the American past tells us, if we invert it, about the new breed of American lawyer has been spotted by Sinyard and Turner in Willie's remark about Lincoln — "Great president, lousy lawyer."[9] In a prescient characterization, Whiplash Willie reminds us that ex-lawyer Nixon and the Watergate break-in were on the political horizon. At times, Willie even looks like Nixon.

Using reason rather than magic, Matthau's Willie is also perhaps the modern urban equivalent of the Evil Spirit of Jewish folklore, a demon who makes vice appear to be virtue. "And the funny thing is — she still cares about you,"[10] he tells a wavering Harry, playing upon his continuing love for his ex-wife. Unlike many Wilder projects, *The Fortune Cookie* depends less upon the baggage brought to it by its players and more upon its players becoming their roles. Willie was Matthau's first significant role, and he has made it his own. Stealing the film from the sedentary Lemmon who graciously gave the best role to his friend, Matthau's comic strip character found critics vying for the shrillest accolade. "Actor Matthau is leering, sneering, sniggering, swaggering, popping his optics, slopping his chops" wrote *Time*. "Whiplash Willie, as incarnated by Matthau's dyspeptic frog's countenance, has a crocodile's eye for the main chance, the patience of a leech and a bite like a bear trap when an insurance company crosses his tracks," wrote Alexander Walker.[11] While for Joseph Morgenstern in *Newsweek*, "He is big and bold and less afraid of a close-up camera than any actor alive. His hands are always in motion, as if searching for something to finagle, and he never lets go of a scene until it is finished."[12]

What is at stake in *The Fortune Cookie* is the average free-thinking, caring American male.[13] Harry is just as much a victim of Willie's reasoning as "Consolidated" and the city of Cleveland. Sinyard and Turner have noted the initial metaphor for this tendency in Harry's job as a cameraman shuffled around the field during cold November play-offs. Meanwhile, Willie can call upon 83,000 spectators and many more TV viewers to vouch that Boom Boom did indeed knock Harry off his feet. But what Willie's reasoning fails to take into account is Harry's capacity to care for others. Whilst Harry cannot sleep because of his conscience, Willie thinks it's because of his corset.

What is at fault is a society which can produce a Whiplash Willie. The lawyer wastes no time in spending the money before he gets the check. "Who waits nowadays? — Take the government — when they shoot a billion dollars'-worth of hardware into space you think they pay cash? It's all on Diner's Club."[14] Sinyard and Turner are quick to spot the parallel with Dr. Dreyfuss' castigation of the credit-card culture in *The Apartment*.[15] As already suggested, a clear line of descent can be traced from *Double Indemnity* to *The Apartment* and on to *The Fortune Cookie* in the annals of the American conman's abuse of reason. Willie's tirade on compensation claims in O'Brien, Thompson and Kincaid's smoke-filled office is reminiscent of Barton Keyes' on suicide incidence in Norton's in *Double Indemnity*.

Beneath the funny surface of *The Fortune Cookie* is something of the violence of *Double Indemnity*. Notice the mood of that scene in which Harry wants out and he and Willie almost come to blows. It is the only time when reason threatens to desert the conman. As in *The Fortune Cookie*, the despair of *The Apartment* is that of the little man so mired in the society's corruption that he cannot win without hurting another person. All three films juggle with comedy and tragedy. While witty dialogue sheds light into the darkness of *Double Indemnity* and lightens the desperation of *The Apartment*, the scheme's grip on Harry pushes *The Fortune Cookie* further into darkness. These three films are Wilder's most eloquent commentaries upon a society which has lost its ethical bearings. If *The Apartment* is a "dirty fairy tale,"[16] Willie here subverts a fairy tale. If "Red Riding Hood" (Harry) doesn't keeps his wits about him, he could become "Dead Riding Hood."[17]

The aesthetically beautiful is often used by Wilder as a counterpoint to the more mean-spirited excesses of the society. Sandy's failure as a civilized human being is in some measure reflected in her failure to recognize an American icon — "Whistler's Mother" — even when the wheelchair-bound Harry poses for it. As Zolotow reads the scene, "You become aware of it in a peripheral fashion, and, gradually, as Lemmon rolls around in his wheelchair, you get the point."[18] Zolotow's wording is revealing because it recalls Sandy's gradual recognition. It is a further echo of that integral relationship within Wilder's films between the interior level of plot and the exterior level of artifice. By dramatizing Sandy's reading of this scene, he also dramatizes our reading of his film. At the end of six months, we are told, Sandy was only on page 19 of

The Carpetbaggers. Such a saga of self-service would perhaps appeal to one as self-serving as Sandy. Its status as a trashy best-seller rather than a text of literary merit is even less to her credit. Significantly, we find Harry reading the same book when she returns. It is an implicit acceptance of her outlook and an unconscious admission that he is unable to see her counterfeit emotions for what they are.

Sandy is another of Wilder's wayward women, sister to Phyllis Dietrichson and Lorraine Minosa. Harry was once in love with a Phyllis, and the screenplay's introduction to Sandy seems strikingly reminiscent of Dietrichson: "She is 28, blonde, wears a shortie nightgown. Even with her hair in disarray, and without makeup, there is something very provocative about her — not too much class, but instant sex."[19] Even her name suggests inconstancy. Completely wrapped up in herself, she ignores a news flash about a natural disaster in favor of a linoleum commercial in which she used to sing.[20] Her inability to gracefully take a compliment on her singing when it is given by Boom Boom is a jarring measure of her spite, Wilder pulling in to a tight and unflattering close-up, pushing this unpleasant character's face into the spectator's face. The frustration which marriage to an emotionally dead woman causes Harry is brutally charted. In one scene she invites him to unzip her dress, offering in return to help him with his corset. We are reminded of Phyllis asking Walter if she has her "face on straight"[21] in this most unromantic of Wilderian exchanges. Sandy's latest role in Harry's life is summed up as she empties her handbag in search of her wedding ring: "The junk you women carry around — it's like the inside of a claw machine."[22] Cementing the men's friendship more indissolubly, then, is Harry and Boom Boom's failure with women. Whilst Harry is preyed upon by Sandy, Boom Boom must contend with another blonde, a black girl with a blonde peroxide perm.

If shady rationalist Willie is Cleveland brother to Los Angeles Claims Manager Keyes in the Wilder genealogy, Pur*key* could be *Keyes*' son. The Purkeys are a staple in the America of the endless caper. But whilst the world is full of deceivers, Purkey is irredeemably lost to the extent that he believes all humanity to be irredeemably corrupt. His cold eye lights up only when his slur against Boom Boom has the desired effect. As Farber sees it, Purkey is the "most repulsive character in the film, far slimier than shyster Willie himself. It is the detective, with his bugging devices and hidden cameras, poking genially into the most intimate activities and conversations, who represents to Wilder the most frightful possibilities of our age."[23] In Purkey, Wilder defined the cinematic prototype of the surveillance technician, a key figure in the paranoid era through which the society was about to pass. It is easy to see in him the blueprint for Harry Caul in Coppola's *The Conversation* of 1974. Sneaking through the film in a cheap raincoat, the chubby Purkey is also the driven city cousin to gas station songsmith Barney Millsap in *Kiss Me, Stupid*.

Foregrounding its structure with titles — "The Caper," "The Return of Tinker Bell," "The Taste of Money" — which seem reminiscent of TV episodes, and peopled by characters with labels rather than names — Gingrich, Hinkle, Purkey, Ferret-Faced Nurse — *The Fortune Cookie* is Wilder and Diamond's final definitive screenplay. Notice how each episode, like a theatrical act, seems to end naturally where the performances end. And notice the signature themes; lugubrious and furtive for Willie, bluesy for Boom Boom. If *Kiss Me, Stupid*'s experiment with form had risked insulting the audience by failing to protect it from ugly characters and their devices, here we never lose sight of the society being lampooned. On the one hand, not since *Double Indemnity* had Wilder described the world so thoroughly as pure plot. On the other, few of his screenplays have discoursed so transparently upon his concerns and professional fortunes.

Most of Wilder's films of the '60s were shot against the grain, and in the age of color TV and glossy movies, *The Fortune Cookie* too was shot with a Panavision lens and in black-and-white. The dichotomy between Good and Evil is present in every corner of the frame. Sharp white for Harry's corset, Boom Boom's Cadillac and the glaring hospital wards. Pitch black for Willie, and off-white for the Mustang he buys Harry. At the end, Harry returns to the deserted, naturally-lit stadium at night,[24] and it feels as though he is fleeing into another film. In the second of Wilder's films with Lemmon and Matthau — *The Front Page* — Wilder returned to the world of the City Desk in the '20s where his professional life had begun.

14

The Front Page

Wilder's remake of Howard Hawks' newspaper classic *His Girl Friday* is a tribute to the American 1920s, a love letter to the Hollywood dialogue tradition which Wilder helped shape, and a revival of the glistening chemistry between Jack Lemmon and Walter Matthau. But, as affectionate as it is, this version[1] is the darkest take on the Ben Hecht-Charles MacArthur play yet.

Appearing in 1974, a year after what is perhaps the archetypal nostalgia movie of a nostalgic decade — *The Sting* — its producer, Universal, hired Wilder and Diamond once Lemmon and Matthau had been secured for the leads. It was their first film away from the Mirisch Corporation for whom Wilder had produced, co-written and directed all his films since *Some Like It Hot*. Sharing Henry Bumstead's period art direction with *The Sting*, and steeped in a plethora of references from the Valentine's Day Massacre to "Lucky Lindy," *The Front Page* in style and spirit seems to collapse both prewar decades into one recollection.[2] Its staccato dialogue and restless thrust revisiting the madcap excess of *Some Like It Hot*, *The Front Page* seemed a natural for Wilder.

But the film met neither box office success nor critical favor. Much of the disfavor revolved around what was perceived as a coarsening of an American theatrical evergreen to cater to the contemporary cinematic sensibility. If *The Sting* had employed pastel-colored conceit to distance its audience from the real implications of its violence and corruption, the polemical Wilder's bitter dialogue and socio-political relevance showed too indiscreetly between the lines. From the dirty glasses and ashtrays strewn over that poker table in the pressroom, to the ominous blood stain on the floor of the Criminal Courts Building, Wilder's film looks lived-in. But what most offended was that Wilder and Diamond used Hollywood's nostalgia fetish as a Trojan horse in which to import a less than savory portrait of today. *The Front Page* is not about he '20s. It is about the '70s.

The curtain went up on the play in 1928, the year Wilder quit journalism for the movies. In keeping with the mid–1970s curiosity about the past, Wilder's film revels in the clutter of the period. The American poster features the *Chicago Examiner*'s Walter Burns in waistcoat and felt hat clasping a period upright phone while star writer Hildy Johnson in a boater taps way on an ancient Remington, a propeller fan swinging above them. In bold black type beneath appear the names "Jack Lemmon and Walter Matthau," with "in a Billy Wilder Film" the only other credit to appear near the title. The whiff of a sure-fire formula must have been hard to resist (a phenomenon which the film itself will dramatize). At the base of the poster appears the recommendation — "Holiday Fun — Now at Movie Theaters Everywhere." In retrospect, it looks like a forlorn attempt to sell the American public a harmless period piece during a Christmas season when all was not well with America.

At one point Burns uses Watergate felon John Ehrlichman's words to describe condemned anarchist Earl Williams' body "twisting slowly, slowly in the wind." Sinyard and Turner are quick to enumerate the many references to the troubled era which inform the film. Indeed, the stench of America's most renowned modern scandal permeates the smoke-filled rooms of Wilder's adaptation. The prospect of a city government rotten from the Mayor on down does recall the second Nixon administration. Notice the photograph of fellow Republican Herbert Hoover in Sheriff Hartman's office. As Sinyard and Turner see it, the cover-up, in which the Illinois Governor's messenger with Williams' reprieve is sent to a brothel by the Mayor which is subsequently raided by police, recalls the Watergate scenario— engineered by the White House and bungled by subordinates. Pauline Kael noticed that Vincent Gardenia's venal Sheriff resembles Chicago Mayor Richard Daley, who brought in the National Guard to quell a Vietnam demonstration at the tragic 1968 Democratic National Convention.

When Walter Burns goes to the Balaban and Katz Theater to persuade Hildy's fiancée not to marry him, he masquerades as a probation officer named Fishbein,[3] there to reveal that Hildy is guilty of exposing himself to school children. Not only does the allegation resonate in an even less innocent era with current paranoia over the child molester, but his parting shot, that he is off to supervise the "Candy Man," carries reminders of the reviled 1992 screen demon of that name. Updated with not a curse or drop of blood wasted, *The Front Page* is a darkening mirror of audience expectations. How fitting, therefore, that Hildy should wish to flee Chicago and Burns for Peggy and Philadelphia, City of Brotherly Love.

"I always play Wilder, Wilder sees me as Wilder — a lovable rogue full of razor blades."[4] Elaborating upon the manipulative best buddy to Lemmon's dopey Good Schlemiel essayed in *The Fortune Cookie*, Matthau's Walter directs Lemmon's Hildy as surely as ever Wilder directed his actors. This Lemmon-Matthau magic is at the heart of *The Front Page*. Wilder has compared Lemmon and Matthau with Redford and Newman. He need not have done so. *The Front Page* is probably Wilder's last best film because its themes — the congame, American popular culture — are so Wilderian, and because this teaming is on such top form. At the point when Hildy tumbles on the phone to 'Fishbein's' ruse, he describes Burns to Peggy as having "mean little eyes and a nose like a pickle." This is almost a word-for-word echo of Wilder's description of Matthau. The line has the feel of an in-joke between the three men. True to the Wilderian tradition of buddies united by professional pride and fear of women, Walter and Hildy not only reply to a craze but apotheosize the most endearing buddy arrangement of the period. In Walter and Hildy, slob and aesthete, man and woman, father and son, and antagonist and protagonist come together. In all of the films which Wilder made with Lemmon and Matthau, there is a degree of malice about the Matthau character which threatens to compromise the Good Schlemiel. On the other hand, the Good Schlemiel can never quite deny the promise of collaboration with the Evil Spirit. This is the essential tension between Matthau and Lemmon. It is perhaps possible to read this threat as a metaphor for the ugly spectre of homosexuality in mainstream cinema. It is also possible to read it in line with a post-war world growing darker by the decade. There is enough of a Wilderian precedent — Keyes/Walter, Chuck/Herbie, Barney/Orville — to read the relationship as the most fully realized example. There was too enough of the uncomplicated stuff of masculine camaraderie for this odd couple to find widespread favor among a mainstream audience.

The harried archetype of American Urban Man reworked by Lemmon throughout the '60s and '70s is crisply evoked in the scene in which, simultaneously tracked by Walter and Peggy to the pressroom, Hildy juggles with receivers while struggling with perennial conflicts —

The oddest couple. Editor Walter Burns (Walter Matthau) and protégé Hildy John-son (Jack Lemmon) contemplate the nature of petty larceny and high-level cor-ruption in *The Front Page.*

Organization Man vs. Husband, Swinging Bachelor vs. Suburban Schlemiel. The scene is a throwback to that in which C. C. Baxter jug-gles clients in *The Apartment.* It is the struggle for Lemmon's soul in a film belonging, as Sinyard and Turner realize, to the darkest side of Wilder's oeuvre. Driven by the latest scoop, the writer in Hildy, like the novelist in Don Birnam, the screenwriter in Joe Gillis, the journalist in Chuck Tatum, will tear himself apart out of pride in his profession. Contrary to Sinyard and Turner's reading, however, Hildy's sickness is not this compulsive attitude. An ex-journalist who has relished memo-ries of Viennese and Berliner days bashing out stories, Wilder has noth-ing but sympathy for the trials through which their professions have put his writer protagonists, and nothing but admiration for the ruses by which they overcome. When Walter scorns the advertising copy his "dumb sonofabitch bastard" plans to leave him for — "I'd walk a mile for a Camel" — we hear the hack's contempt for the meaningless jingles that fill the American airwaves. Lifted from Wilder's store of Tin Pan Alley memories, and resonant with the conflicting allegiances here, the lyrics to *You Belong to Me* sung by Peggy at the picture house also have the trite ring of cheap copy. Walter might also scorn writing for the movies or writing the Great American Novel, but Wilder's point is clear. You do what you can do, and stick with it. Like the film director, the professional journalist must keep getting it up, no matter how often he or she is led astray.

What Wilder needed after *The Private Life of Sherlock Holmes* and *Avanti!* flopped was "a great fat hit."[5] Notice that Walter extends Hildy the promise of graduating into the same league as H. L. Mencken with the Earl Williams story. Meanwhile, the other hacks in the pressroom comfort themselves with sensationalist and peripheral stories. In Walter's struggle to keep Hildy up to the mark resonates Wilder and Diamond's struggle to reiterate their acumen in '70s Hollywood, turning the gimmickry — the buddy movie, the nostalgia craze — of the moment to their own account. In their epilogue, Hildy, having departed the *Examiner* with Peggy, eventually returns. Old Hacks die hard. In *The Front Page* Wilder dramatizes the fate of the artist in a consumer society — compelled to make a living, but driven to make a difference.

The "unseen power" which Walter claims looks after the *Examiner* chimes with the privileged view which Burns and Johnson have of the city and the privileged access which they have to the Big Story. While the other hacks run around pursuing inconsequential copy, and whore Mollie Malloy rails against them for ridiculing her and Williams, they seeks nothing less than to kick over City Hall "like an apple cart." This wider perspective in turn chimes with Wilder's position as director of the actors and of the events we watch. In criticizing *The Front Page*, Pauline Kael claimed that, whereas His *Girl Friday* has verbal precision, Wilder's version reduces the play to a lot of hollering. But it is Lemmon and Matthau's lines which we hear and remember. It is the pressroom hacks whose dialogue overlaps, and whose differing takes on events seem shrill and over-smart. This is Lemmon, Matthau and Wilder's story. The peripheral characters, in retrospect, read like a roll call of '60s Wilder bit parts and '70s American film and TV fauna.

Emerging from the Chicago streets is Doro Merande as Jennie, the cleaner at the Criminal Courts Building. It is a haunting closure to the scene when she silently appears and genuflects as Williams is led away. Wilder regular Noam Pitlik plays Wilson, one of the pressroom boys. Cliff Osmond turns up as city lackey Police Captain Jacobi. Martin Gabel plays possibly the most cartoonish of Wilder's shrinks in Dr Eggelhofer. Austin Pendleton makes the bookish little convict into a version of the poor schnook made famous during this period by Woody Allen in such as *Take the Money and Run* (1969) and *Sleeper* (1973). The anarchist once mailed a bomb in a shoe box to J. P. Morgan. It was returned due to insufficient postage, and blew the roof off his house. It could be an Allen anecdote.

Carol Burnett's Mollie Malloy is the angry center of *The Front Page*. Critics have said that she unbalances the film, but Wilder needs her passion to make the decline in standards, which he dramatizes, stick. Sinyard and Turner show that, if we are laughing at the press boys' crude jokes about her and her relationship with Williams, when she spits at them the camera is so placed that she is spitting at us. Later, she spits at them again before leaping from the pressroom window. But now the camera is alongside her looking back at them. That the mob of hacks appear to drive Mollie to the window with their taunts effectively makes them accomplices to her attempted suicide. Wilder is clearly in sympathy with this character and her tirades against these unprincipled second-raters. In this light, any claim that *The Front Page* is no more than a meditation upon giving the public what it wants is an oversimplification.

Peggy is the latest in a long line of sweet-natured female dopes in Wilder which stretches from Emmy Brown to Zelda Spooner. Played by Susan Sarandon, a charming actor who has since excelled at embattled fortitude, the final insult is that, although Hildy left her, she named a child after him. Clearly, it was a blow tantamount to dashing Sugar's hopes or abandoning Fran Kubelik.

Played by the grizzled likes of Charles Durning, Allen Garfield and Herb Edelman, these "crazy buttinskis with dandruff on their shoulders and holes in their pants, gray-haired, hump-backed, half blind, bumming cigarettes from office boys and peeping through keyholes" represent the "worst element" of the tabloid tradition. If Burns and Johnson are in a higher league, this mob recall the impotents lured to Escudero by Chuck Tatum's success. David Wayne's poet-hack Bensinger is a damning indictment of the slippage of standards. (He would also see off those who wish to read homosexual intent into Lemmon and Matthau's relationship.)

But for all of its mud-slinging and blood stained floors, *The Front Page* is also a rollicking Wilder entertainment. Like *The Spirit of St. Louis* and *Some Like It Hot*, it misses no opportunity to revel in the age. The opening scene, as recollected by Geoff Brown, is a miracle of energetic imagery and pacy cutting. "While the credits roll to jazz accompaniment, typesetters feverishly lock the letters into place and drums of paper are fixed to the printing press, the bell sounds, all systems are go, and a new edition of the *Chicago Examiner*, clatters into life; a copy is snatched from the conveyor belt and its front page assessed, the camera closing in on the leading article (the hanging of anarchist Earl Williams)."[6]

The sense in which Wilder remembers is reflected in the many references to '20s icons from Commander Byrd to Sacco and Vanzetti. It is reflected on another level in the references to Wilder's own evocations of the era. When Hildy is first seen, he wanders into the *Examiner* offices among the clatter of typewriters, reminding us of that opening among the hacks at the hotel before the Lindbergh flight. In what is one of the best belly laughs in a Wilder film, the stretcher bearing Dr. Eggelhoffer leaves the back of the ambulance and runs untended down the middle of a city street, Eggelhoffer screaming to be admitted to a Viennese hospital. Police cars with officers on the running boards careen through Chicago in Keystone Kops style, evoking the fury of *Some Like It Hot*. What that Christmas audience didn't fully appreciate when they bought into Wilder's past was that the ex-newspaperman always knew a good story when he saw one.

15

Buddy Buddy

From a film-historical standpoint, *The Front Page* is the most interesting Wilder film of his late period because it dramatizes his beginnings in journalism and, more obliquely, it dramatizes the fate of the older film director in the Hollywood of the Movie Brats. It is a film which is indirectly about the genesis of one of classical American cinema's auteurs. A much lesser film, *Buddy Buddy* is nevertheless significant for dramatizing Wilder's growing sense of redundancy.

By the late late 1970s, Wilder and Diamond were finding projects harder and harder to finance. *Buddy Buddy* originated as a French boulevard farce entitled *L'Emmerdeur (A Pain in the A —)* directed by Edouard Molinaro and released in 1973. Having secured the American rights, producers Alain Bernheim and Jay Weston managed to interest Jack Lemmon and Walter Matthau in the roles originally played by Lino Ventura and Jacques Brel. Lemmon and Matthau in turn interested Wilder and Diamond enough to write a treatment. *Buddy Buddy* was released in 1981 to bad and disappointing reviews.

Times have moved on since the early 1980s and so, paradoxically, the film does not now offend quite so much. Playing out a series of misunderstandings in a hotel in southern California, *Buddy Buddy* often seems reminiscent of *Avanti!* and looks back to the beginnings of Wilder's career and that hotel on the Mexican border in *Hold Back the Dawn*. Looking like a rerun of *The Odd Couple*, and full of swipes at '60s fads from sex clinics to *Love Story*, as the years go by, the swipes seem less miscalculated, the film looking and sounding increasingly as though made around 1973.

At one point, Walter Matthau's misanthropic Mafia hitman Trabucco and Jack Lemmon's neurotic TV censor Victor Clooney pick up a pair of hippies just as the woman of the pair is about to give birth. As an allusion to the culture of free love, it is inaccurate; he would never call his son "Elvis." But it's the couple in the front who interest Wilder and Diamond. *Buddy Buddy* is the third film in Wilder's oeuvre to star Lemmon and Matthau and, as its title suggests, the first to revolve consciously around the duo as an institution. The "buddy movie" emerged in the late 1960s and flowered in the mid–1970s, in significant part thanks to Wilder and Diamond. But whereas Harry Hinkle left "Whiplash Willie" in *The Fortune Cookie* and Hildy Johnson left Walter Burns in *The Front Page*, (reportedly returning in the epilogue), here the couple end the film together, sequestered on a desert island.

Film-historically, *Buddy Buddy* is interesting because of this ending. Without knowing it, Wilder anticipated such mistakes as *Grumpy Old Men* (1993) and *The Odd Couple II* (1997), dramatizing the redundancy of Lemmon and Matthau, a box office item which he and Diamond had created. Confronted with post–Kinsey sexual abandon at Dr. Zuckerbrot's sex clinic, Lemmon's middle-aged middle-class square can only retreat into indignant despair. Confronted with the lovelorn Victor, Trabucco can only do what Matthau's evil spirit has always done; implicate Lemmon in a guilty world, this time by handing him a rifle to carry out Trabucco's final commission. Having fulfilled their remits for Wilder, the couple retreat to their place in the sun, forgotten men. Having made enough in the "pest control" racket to buy the island, Trabucco is last seen, surrounded by Polynesian servants, smoking a cigar and watching a football game. When Victor arrives and his boat breaks up on the rocks, he resignedly tells a voluptuous maiden that he'll be staying for dinner, and supper, and breakfast, and dinner.... As tasteless as *Buddy Buddy* often is, there is something knowing about this ending which now seems oddly appropriate to Wilder's career.

What most disappoints can perhaps be summed up in Trabucco's dilemma. Plagued by pain-in-the-ass Victor, he simply wants to do an honest day's work. It is precisely that lack of a more substantial agenda which sabotages the film. Whether it was the nature of guilt (*Double Indemnity*), fame (*Sunset Blvd.*), the work ethic (*The Front Page*), Wilder's films have always had big themes to worry over. Here it looks as though the screenwriters simply wanted to work again, making Joe Baltake's comment *Buddy Buddy* is from hunger"[1] oddly poignant, paraphrasing as it does script girl Betty Schaefer's put-down of Joe Gillis in *Sunset Blvd.* Lacking a coherent axe to grind, *Buddy Buddy* vainly tries to reanimate a classic Wilderian situation — the delinquent pro hampered by his moral conscience — for the "dating audience"[2] of the '80s, a constituency Diamond scathes for its illiteracy. "They wandered up and down the aisles, talked with their friends and so on. In other words, the connective tissue of movies no longer interests them. They watch television in fifteen-minute chunks with a climax and they aren't interested in following a plot."[3] Ironically, a discrete quality also afflicts *Buddy Buddy*, making you want to tune in and out. It is a film of moments and parts which, lacking anything new to say, flails blindly at contemporary manners and mores. It is a film by old men disappointed over losing their audience.

Yet Wilder and Diamond's polemic is not without precedent or point. "I have not wavered as to which country I wanted to be a citizen of — never. I thought it was great — the energy, the generosity, even with all the foibles, the human weaknesses."[4] As *Buddy Buddy* begins, the camera is focused on a stand of palm trees on a suburban California street, the Panavision lens making them appear (on television) elongated, while Lalo Schifrin's tinny score makes a sad plea for acceptance

Old men disappointed over losing their audience. *Left to right,* Victor Clooney (Jack Lemmon) and Trabucco (Walter Matthau) trade gripes in *Buddy Buddy.*

in the era of electronica. That street could be yucca-lined Los Feliz Boulevard along which Walter Neff drives to Phyllis Dietrichson's mock–Spanish lounge. Those naked trunks recall the voluptuous legs of the chorines behind Dino at the beginning of *Kiss Me, Stupid*. *Buddy Buddy*'s asides at the '60s may date the film, but his critique of American excess seems as eager as ever. On the back of the dairy truck adopted by Trabucco as a cover for an assassination is the slogan "Feel Better, Live Longer." A characteristically black Wilder touch. But also very characteristic of the trite "Smiley badge" culture, one which finds store clerks from Bangor, Maine, to Honolulu wishing you well with the litany "Have a nice day." On two occasions, Trabucco is persuaded to spend more when all he wants is a cigar at a concession stand. Wilder's point is that the blanding down of commercial exchange somewhere along the line deletes the individual's own personality and predilections. Such a complaint goes hand-in-hand with his observation that, by the late 1960s, film directors have to spend 80 percent of their time wheeling and dealing and only 20 percent actually making films. Diamond's railing against television viewing habits is here seen in context. Clearly, Wilder feels that such a world no longer has a place for Trabucco's, or Wilder's, ideas about craftsmanship.

When he arrives at the Ramona Hotel in Riverside,[5] Trabucco meticulously secures his room against interference, assembles his rifle, and sets up his tripod in preparation for the job at hand. We are reminded of Walter's preparations to kill Dietrichson in *Double Indemnity*. Then Victor begins his first suicide attempt next door. If Trabucco is Wilder, Victor represents his worst bugbear. A prude who is unable to stomach any of the corruptions to which weak humanity is prone, he epitomizes the worst kind of consensual American hypocrisy. From Will Hays' condemning *Double Indemnity*'s murderous blueprint to the Dallas Motion Picture Censorship Board's picking Wilder up for bad language in *The Front Page*, the censor has dogged the filmmaker. The moment when Victor discovers that his estranged wife Celia's wedding ring has been melted down and now hangs as a gold penis around Zuckerbrot's neck is crude. But, for Wilder, Clooney's shocked response: "The (p) word!!" is cruder. The distinction embodied in Trabucco and Clooney is the distinction between the artist whose duty it is to push out the boundaries of what is acceptable, and the moral guardian whose ill-informed guess is to staunch his or her creativity. If Zuckerbrot's clinic seems cartoonish, with Klaus Kinski Wilder's crassest take on European medical science yet, and Mrs. Clooney a pale copy of Paula Prentiss as the perennial '60s neurotic, in the unholy alliance between Trabucco and Clooney can be felt forces which have pushed and pulled Wilder since *The Major and the Minor*. But as *Buddy Buddy*'s excessive energy suggests, only someone as simultaneously inside and outside the system as Wilder could have rounded off his American oeuvre in a manner both passionate and rebellious.

Filmography

Cast and credits are provided only for films discussed in this book.

EUROPE

1929

Menschen am Sonntag/People on Sunday (screenwriter)

1931

Der Mann, der seinen Mörder sucht/Looking for His Murderer (co-screenwriter)

Der Falsche Ehemann/The Counterfeit Husband (co-screenwriter)

Ihre Hoheit Befiehlt/Her Majesty Commands (co-screenwriter)

Emil und die Detective/Emil and the Detectives (screenwriter)

1932

Es war einmal ein Waltzer/Once Upon a Time There Was a Waltz (screenwriter)

Ein Blonder Traum/A Blonde Dream (co-screenwriter)

Ein Mädel der Strasse/A Girl of the Street (co-screenwriter)

Das Blaue vom Himmel/The Blue from Heaven (co-screenwriter)

1933

Madame wunscht keine Kinder/Madame Wants No Children (co-screen-writer)

Was Frauen Träumen/What Women Dream (co-screenwriter)

Mauvaise Graine/Bad Seed (co-director)

UNITED STATES

1934

Music in the Air (co-screenwriter)

1935

Lottery Lover (co-screenwriter)

1938

Bluebeard's Eighth Wife (co-screenwriter)

1939

Midnight (co-screenwriter)

What a Life (co-screenwriter)

Ninotchka (co-screenwriter)

1940

Arise, My Love (co-screenwriter)

1941

Hold Back the Dawn
    Paramount Pictures
    PRODUCER: Arthur Hornblow Jr.
    DIRECTOR: Mitchell Leisen
    SCREENPLAY: Charles Brackett and Billy Wilder
    PHOTOGRAPHY: Leo Tover
    EDITING: Doane Harrison
    MUSIC: Victor Young

LEADING PLAYERS: Charles Boyer (Georges Iscovescu), Olivia de Havilland (Emmy Brown), Paulette Goddard (Anita Dixon), Victor Francen (Van den Leucken).
115 mins. B/W.

Ball of Fire
Goldwyn Productions
PRODUCER: Samuel Goldwyn
DIRECTOR: Howard Hawks
SCREENPLAY: Charles Brackett and Billy Wilder
PHOTOGRAPHY: Leo Tover
EDITING: Daniel Mandell
MUSIC: Alfred Newman
LEADING PLAYERS: Gary Cooper (Professor Bertram Potts), Barbara Stanwyck (Sugarpuss O'Shea), Oscar Homolka (Professor Gurkakoff), S. Z. Sakall (Professor Magenbruch).
112 mins. B/W.

1942

The Major and the Minor
Paramount Pictures
PRODUCER: Arthur Hornblow Jr.
DIRECTOR: Billy Wilder
SCREENPLAY: Charles Brackett and Billy Wilder
PHOTOGRAPHY: Leo Tover
EDITING: Doane Harrison
MUSIC: Robert Emmett Dolan
LEADING PLAYERS: Ginger Rogers (Susan Applegate), Ray Milland (Major Kirby), Rita Johnson (Pamela Hill), Robert Benchley (Mr. Osborne).
101 mins. B/W.

1943

Five Graves to Cairo (director/co-screenwriter)

1944

Double Indemnity
Paramount Pictures
PRODUCER: Joseph Sistrom
DIRECTOR: Billy Wilder
SCREENPLAY: Billy Wilder and Raymond Chandler

PHOTOGRAPHY: John F. Seitz
EDITING: Doane Harrison
MUSIC: Miklós Rózsa
LEADING PLAYERS: Fred MacMurray (Walter Neff), Barbara Stanwyck (Phyllis Dietrichson), Edward G. Robinson (Barton Keyes), Jean Heather (Lola Dietrichson).
107 mins. B/W.

1945

The Lost Weekend
Paramount Pictures
PRODUCER: Charles Brackett
DIRECTOR: Billy Wilder
SCREENPLAY: Charles Brackett and Billy Wilder
PHOTOGRAPHY: John F. Seitz
EDITING: Doane Harrison
MUSIC: Miklós Rózsa
LEADING PLAYERS: Ray Milland (Don Birnam), Jane Wyman (Helen St. James), Howard da Silva (Nat), Phillip Terry (Wick Birnam).
99 mins. B/W.

1947

The Emperor Waltz (director/co-screenwriter)

1948

A Foreign Affair (director/co-screenwriter)

1950

Sunset Blvd.
Paramount Pictures
PRODUCER: Charles Brackett
DIRECTOR: Billy Wilder
SCREENPLAY: Charles Brackett, Billy Wilder and D. M. Marshman, Jr.
PHOTOGRAPHY: John F. Seitz
EDITING: Doane Harrison and Arthur Schmidt
MUSIC: Franz Waxman
LEADING PLAYERS: William Holden (Joe Gillis), Gloria Swanson (Norma Desmond), Erich Von Stroheim (Max Von Mayerling), Nancy Olson (Betty Schaefer).
110 mins. B/W.

1951

Ace in the Hole/The Big Carnival
    Paramount Pictures
    PRODUCER: Billy Wilder
    DIRECTOR: Billy Wilder
    SCREENPLAY: Billy Wilder, Lesser Samuels and Walter Newman
    PHOTOGRAPHY: Charles B. Lang, Jr.
    EDITING: Arthur Schmidt
    MUSIC: Hugo Friedhofer
    LEADING PLAYERS: Kirk Douglas (Chuck Tatum), Jan Sterling (Lorraine), Bob Arthur (Herbie Cook), Porter Hall (Jacob Q. Boot).
    111 mins. B/W.

1953

Stalag 17
    Paramount Pictures
    PRODUCER: Billy Wilder
    DIRECTOR: Billy Wilder
    SCREENPLAY: Billy Wilder and Edwin Blum
    PHOTOGRAPHY: Ernest Laszlo
    EDITING: George Tomasini
    MUSIC: Franz Waxman
    LEADING PLAYERS: William Holden (Sefton), Don Taylor (Lt. Dunbar), Robert Strauss ("Animal"), Harvey Lembeck (Harry).
    121 mins. B/W.

1954

Sabrina/Sabrina Fair (director/co-screenwriter)

1955

The Seven Year Itch
    20th Century–Fox/Feldman Group Productions
    PRODUCER: Charles K. Feldman and Billy Wilder
    DIRECTOR: Billy Wilder
    SCREENPLAY: Billy Wilder and George Axelrod
    PHOTOGRAPHY: Milton Krasner
    EDITING: Hugh B. Fowler
    MUSIC: Alfred Newman
    LEADING PLAYERS: Marilyn Monroe (The Girl), Tom Ewell (Richard Sherman), Evelyn Keyes (Helen Sherman), Sonny Tufts (Tom Mackenzie).
    105 mins. DeLuxe Color/Cinemascope.

1957

The Spirit of St. Louis
Warner Brothers
PRODUCER: Leland Hayward
DIRECTOR: Billy Wilder
SCREENPLAY: Billy Wilder and Wendell Mayes
PHOTOGRAPHY: Robert Burks and J. Peverall Marley
EDITING: Arthur Schmidt
MUSIC: Franz Waxman
LEADING PLAYERS: James Stewart (Charles Lindbergh), Murray Hamilton (Bud Gurney), Patricia Smith (Mirror Girl), Bartlett Robinson (B. F. Mahoney).
134 mins. Warner Color.

Love in the Afternoon (director/co-screenwriter)

1958

Witness for the Prosecution (director/co-screenwriter)

1959

Some Like it Hot
Mirisch Productions
PRODUCER: Billy Wilder
DIRECTOR: Billy Wilder
SCREENPLAY: Billy Wilder and I. A. L. Diamond
PHOTOGRAPHY: Charles B. Lang, Jr.
EDITING: Arthur Schmidt
MUSIC: Adolph Deutsch
LEADING PLAYERS: Marilyn Monroe ("Sugar Kane"), Tony Curtis (Joe), Jack Lemmon (Jerry), George Raft ("Spats" Columbo).
122 mins. B/W.

1960

The Apartment
Mirisch Productions
PRODUCER: Billy Wilder
DIRECTOR: Billy Wilder
SCREENPLAY: Billy Wilder and I. A. L. Diamond
PHOTOGRAPHY: Joseph LaShelle
EDITING: Daniel Mandell

Music: Adolph Deutsch
Leading Players: Jack Lemmon (C. C. Baxter), Shirley MacLaine (Fran Kubelik), Fred MacMurray (J. D. Sheldrake), Ray Walston (Mr Dobisch).
125 mins. B/W. Panavision.

1961

One, Two, Three (director/co-screenwriter)

1963

Irma La Douce (director/co-screenwriter)

1964

Kiss Me, Stupid
    Mirisch/Phalanx Productions
    Producer: Billy Wilder
    Director: Billy Wilder
    Screenplay: Billy Wilder and I. A. L. Diamond
    Photography: Joseph LaShelle
    Editing: Daniel Mandell
    Music: André Previn and George and Ira Gershwin
    Leading Players: Dean Martin (Dino), Kim Novak (Polly the Pistol), Ray Walston (Orville J. Spooner), Felicia Farr (Zelda Spooner).
    124 mins. B/W. Panavision.

1966

The Fortune Cookie/Meet Whiplash Willie
    Mirisch/Phalanx/Jalem Productions
    Producer: Billy Wilder
    Director: Billy Wilder
    Screenplay: Billy Wilder and I. A. L. Diamond
    Photography: Joseph LaShelle
    Editing: Daniel Mandell
    Music: Andre Previn
    Leading Players: Jack Lemmon (Harry Hinkle), Walter Matthau (Willie Gingrich), Ron Rich ("Boom Boom" Jackson), Cliff Osmond (Purkey).
    125 mins. B/W. Panavision.

1970

The Private Life of Sherlock Holmes (director/co-screenwriter)

1972

Avanti! (director/co-screenwriter)

1974

The Front Page
Universal Pictures
Producer: Paul Monash
Director: Billy Wilder
Screenplay: Billy Wilder and I. A. L. Diamond
Photography: Jordan Cronenweth
Editing: Ralph E. Winters
Music: Billy May
Leading Players: Jack Lemmon (Hildy Johnson), Walter Matthau (Walter Burns), Carol Burnett (Molly Malloy), Allen Garfield (Kruger).
105 mins. Technicolor. Panavision.

1979

Fedora (director/co-screenwriter)

1981

Buddy Buddy
Metro-Goldwyn-Mayer
PRODUCER: Jay Weston
DIRECTOR: Billy Wilder
SCREENPLAY: Billy Wilder and I. A. L. Diamond
PHOTOGRAPHY: Harry Stradling, Jr.
EDITING: Argyle Nelson
MUSIC: Lalo Schifrin
LEADING PLAYERS: Jack Lemmon (Victor Clooney), Walter Matthau (Trabucco), Paula Prentiss (Celia Clooney), Klaus Kinski (Dr. Zuckerbrot).
96 mins. MetroColor. Panavision.

Notes

Introduction

1. Quoted in Zolotow, *Billy Wilder in Hollywood*, 55.
2. Sinyard and Turner, *Journey Down Sunset Blvd.*, vii.
3. Baxter, *Hollywood in the Thirties*, 33–34.
4. *Ibid.*, 42.
5. Sarris, "Billy Wilder: Closet Romanticist," *Film Comment*, July-August, 1976, 8.
6. Quoted in Willett, "Billy Wilder's *A Foreign Affair* (1945–1948): The Trials and Tribulations of Berlin," *Historical Journal of Film, Radio and Television*, Volume 7, Number 1, 1987, 13–14.
7. Stam, "Fedora," *Cineaste*, Winter, 1979, 56.

Chapter 1

1. Dick, *Billy Wilder*, 26.
2. Sinyard and Turner, *Journey Down Sunset Blvd.*, 119.
3. By 1941, Chevrolet sales had exceeded even Ford's, making it the top manufacturer on the American market. Emmy's station wagon was thus the archetypal American vehicle of that year.
4. Quoted in McBride and McCarthy, "Going for Extra Innings," *Film Comment*, January-February, 1979, 47.

Chapter 2

1. Quoted in Dick, *Billy Wilder*, 162.
2. Quoted in Anobile, *Ernst Lubitsch's Ninotchka*, 12.

3. Brackett quoted in Luft, "Two Views of a Director — Billy Wilder," *Quarterly of Film, Radio and TV*, Autumn, 1952, 67.

4. In the Nabokov book, Humbert marries Charlotte Haze so as to be near "Little Lo."

Chapter 3

1. Nichols and Gassner, *Best Film Plays of 1945*, 123.

2. Schickel, *Double Indemnity*, 9.

3. Dick, *Billy Wilder*, 195.

4. Nichols and Gassner, *Best Film Plays of 1945*, 132.

5. Farber, "The Films of Billy Wilder," *Film Comment*, Winter, 1971-72, 11.

6. Nichols and Gassner, *Best Film Plays of 1945*, 133.

7. Seidman, *Billy Wilder*, 36.

8. Nichols and Gassner, *Best Film Plays of 1945*, 133.

9. *Ibid.*, 131.

10. Phyllis tells Walter that Dietrichson once returned home from a party and sat in the garage with the engine running. Arguably, straightened dynamics operate throughout the screenplay, this marriage making victims of both characters.

11. John Henley quoted in Museum of the Moving Image programme notes for a June, 1989 screening.

12. Crowther, *Double Indemnity*, 11 September, 1944.

13. Nichols and Gassner, *Best Film Plays of 1945*, 131.

14. *Ibid.*, 126.

15. *Ibid.*, 171.

16. *Ibid.*, 171.

17. *Ibid.*, 170.

18. An obvious allusion to Marlene Dietrich, the key femme fatale of the Weimar '20s and the Paramount '30s.

19. Nichols and Gassner, *Best Film Plays of 1945*, 125.

20. *Ibid.*, 174.

21. One is reminded of Richard Conte's leaning on his friend for a smoke in Lewis Milestone's 1946 *A Walk in the Sun*. His line: "It pays to have friends." Sinyard and Turner point to similarly supportive routines in the all-male groups of Hawks' films.

22. Tyler, *Magic and Myth of the Movies*, 236.

23. Even the name "Keyes" suggests a walking tool for detection, whilst "Neff" could be read as a translation of "naif."

24. Sarris, *Billy Wilder: Closet Romanticist*, 9.

25. Nichols and Gassner, *Best Film Plays of 1945*, 155.

26. Schickel, *Double Indemnity*, 31.

27. Author unknown, *Double Indemnity*, August, 1944, 89.

28. Zolotow, *Billy Wilder in Hollywood*, 117.

29. Tyler, *Magic and Myth of the Movies*, 178.

30. Nichols and Gassner, *Best Film Plays of 1945*, 171.

Chapter 4

1. Quoted in Zolotow, *Billy Wilder in Hollywood*, 321.

Chapter 5

1. Higham, "Meet Whiplash Wilder," 22.
2. Staiger, "The Classical Hollywood Cinema," 128.
3. Brackett, "Two Views of a Director — Billy Wilder," *Quarterly of Film, Radio and TV*, Fall, 1952, 69.
4. Schlondorff, "Billy, How Did You Do It?" *Arena* TV documentary, 1992.
5. Sinyard and Turner, *Journey Down Sunset Blvd.*, 273.
6. Crowther, *The Great Films: 50 Golden Years of Motion Pictures*, 198–200.
7. Quinlan, *Illustrated Directory of Film Stars*, 355.
8. Wilder, in Schlöndorff.
9. Introduced at Paramount in 1947, latensification was used to increase film speed when filming on location. According to Lightman, the method was used for around 15 percent of the filming.
10. Lightman, "Old Master, New Tricks," 318.

Chapter 6

1. Quoted in Halliwell, *Halliwell's Film Guide*, 6.
2. Sinyard and Turner, *Journey Down Sunset Blvd.*, 136.
3. Brackett, "Two Views of a Director — Billy Wilder," 69.
4. Sinyard and Turner, *Journey Down Sunset Blvd.*, 130.
5. McBride and Wilmington, "The Private Life of Billy Wilder," 8.
6. Hall played the lively westerner Jackson in *Double Indemnity*, a hick whose exposure to Los Angeles soon wore down *his* integrity.
7. Sinyard and Turner have noticed, the alliance between Tatum and the trusting Leo foresees that between Hinkle and his "victim" "Boom Boom" Jackson.
8. Dick, *Billy Wilder*, 60.

Chapter 7

1. Sinyard and Turner, National Film Theater program notes, 6.
2. Poague, "The Politics of Perception: Wilder's "Stalag 17," 19–25.
3. In a shrewd casting decision, Wilder ironizes his own position as a "German" director in Hollywood by casting another "German" (both men are actually Austrian in origin), in the role of this languishing Prussian petty tyrant, a variation upon the emasculated Max von Mayerling.

4. Rumann played "Concentration Camp" Erhardt in Lubitsch's *To Be or Not to Be* (1942), a film which was described in *Newsweek* at the time as "having a good time at the expense of Nazi myth" (Halliwell, *Film Guide*, 1057). Rumann was clearly doing the same again, and loving every minute.

Chapter 8

1. Quoted in Gunton, "Billy Wilder 1906– ," 457.
2. Corliss, *Talking Pictures — Screenwriters of Hollywood*, 91.
3. Quoted in Corliss, *ibid.*, 93.
4. *Ibid.*, 90.
5. Quoted in Gunton, "Billy Wilder 1906– ," 457.
6. McCann, *Marilyn Monroe*, 99–100.
7. Co-producing with Wilder was Charles K. Feldman, a short man with red hair and glasses (according to Woody Allen), who also produced Allen's first screenplay *What's New, Pussycat?* In *Breakfast at Tiffany's*, tycoon Rusty Trawler is also short and has red hair and glasses. The genealogical plot thickens.
8. Axelrod quoted in McBride and McCarthy, "Going for Extra Innings," *Film Comment*, January–February, 1979, 44.

Chapter 9

1. Quoted in Zolotow, *Billy Wilder in Hollywood*, 187.
2. Quoted in Eyles, *James Stewart*, 130.
3. Quoted in Zolotow, *Billy Wilder in Hollywood*, 193.
4. Quoted in Higham and Greenberg, *The Celluloid Muse — Hollywood Directors Speak*, 251.
5. Quoted in Zolotow, *Billy Wilder in Hollywood*, 193.
6. Hart, "The Spirit of St. Louis," 128.
7. *Ibid.*, 128.
8. It was Warners which was responsible for classic '30s biopics *The Story of Louis Pasteur*, *Dr. Ehrlich's Magic Bullet* and, in 1950, a tribute to American populist icon Will Rogers.
9. Zolotow, *Billy Wilder in Hollywood*, 193.
10. Hart, "The Spirit of St. Louis," 126.
11. Rowan, "Making the Aerial Shots for *The Spirit of St. Louis*," 366–387.
12. Spiller, "A World of Wilder," 76.
13. Quoted in Eyles, *James Stewart*, 131.
14. It is worth comparing Stewart as Lindbergh with Cooper as Bertram Potts. Both are boffins with an in-built innocence which brooks no compromise, and a determination which will surmount any obstacle.
15. Eyles, *James Stewart*, 132.
16. Sinyard and Turner, *Journey Down Sunset Blvd.*, 353.

Chapter 10

1. Dick, *Billy Wilder*, 88.
2. Sinyard and Turner, *Journey Down Sunset Blvd.*, 228.
3. According to Zolotow (*Billy Wilder in Hollywood*), in 1958 Wilder signed a contract giving him freedom of subject, screenplay, casting, direction, final cut, a good salary as director/screenwriter, and 25 percent of the net profits. He would stay with the Mirisch Brothers for 16 years (Zolotow, 200).
4. Thomson, *A Biographical Dictionary of the Cinema*, 609.
5. McBride and Wilmington, "The Private Life of Billy Wilder," 4.
6. A film which Wilder will remake in 1974 as *The Front Page*.
7. Quoted in Corliss, *Talking Pictures*, 153.
8. Quoted in Baltake, *Jack Lemmon, His Films and Career*, 97.
9. In no other Wilder film since *The Lost Weekend* is drink such an important issue.
10. In this regard, it is worth noting that Wilder shot the Miami sequences not far from Hollywood near San Diego.
11. Zolotow, *Billy Wilder in Hollywood*, 201.
12. *Ibid.*, 201.
13. Turner, "Interview with I. A. L. Diamond," 17–18.
14. Mast, *The Comic Mind*, 276.
15. Dyer, "Some Like It Hot," Wilder, 173.
16. Wilder quoted in Higham and Greenberg, *The Celluloid Muse*, 252.
17. Corliss, *Talking Pictures*, 154.
18. Quoted in Wernblad, *Brooklyn Is Not Expanding*, 19.
19. Quoted in Baltake, *Jack Lemmon, His Films and Career*, 12.
20. Corliss, *Talking Pictures*, 154.
21. "Some Like It Hot," Author unknown, June, 1959, 69.
22. Sinyard and Turner, *Journey Down Sunset Blvd.*, 227.

Chapter 11

1. Wilder and Diamond, *The Apartment*, 88.
2. *Ibid.*, 85.
3. Dick, *Billy Wilder*, 91.
4. Wilder and Diamond, *The Apartment*, 91.
5. *Ibid.*, 13.
6. *Ibid.*, 73.
7. *Ibid.*, 83.
8. A Broadway show about a conman who is confronted with his own humanity.
9. Wilder and Diamond, *The Apartment*, 54.
10. Spiller, "A World of Wilder," 81.
11. Wilder and Diamond, *The Apartment*, 81.

12. *Ibid.*, 72.
13. Nichols and Gassner, *Best Film Plays of 1945*, 142.
14. Wilder and Diamond, *The Apartment*, 51.
15. Dick, *Billy Wilder*, 93.
16. Wilder and Diamond, *The Apartment*, 14.
17. Quoted in Sinyard and Turner, *Journey Down Sunset Blvd.*, 161.
18. Mast, *The Comic Mind*, 275.
19. Wilder and Diamond, *The Apartment*, 33.
20. Sinyard and Turner, *Journey Down Sunset Blvd.*, 157.
21. Lemmon, "Such Fun to Be Funny," 7.
22. Wilder and Diamond, *The Apartment*, 31.
23. Freedland, *Jack Lemmon*, 172.
24. Zolotow, *Billy Wilder in Hollywood*, 309.
25. Quoted in Giannetti, *Masters of the American Cinema*, 13:11.
26. Wilder and Diamond, *The Apartment*, 111.

Chapter 12

1. Quoted in Vizzard, *See No Evil*, 306.
2. Quoted in Sinyard and Turner, *Journey Down Sunset Blvd.*, 248.
3. The name of the farce from which *Kiss Me, Stupid* originated is *L'Ora della Fantasia*. Acknowledging the kernel of fantasy which motivates human sexual experience, this title also chimes with Wilder's examination of the ways in which our experience is shaped in the cinema auditorium. His interrogation of Hollywood sacred cows and the ironic deployment of icon Dean Martin seem to bare the edevices by which mainstream cinema manipulates the spectator. Wilder's *Fantasia* depends upon the spectator's willing complicity in the conventions of the majority fantasy.
4. At one point, Dino, whose fuel line is cut by a Barney anxious to keep him in one place long enough to hear their songs, is towed back into town like Chuck Tatum into Albuquerque. The difference between Dino and Tatum is that what happens to the complex Tatum has an impact on his view of himself and others.
5. Quoted in Zolotow, *Billy Wilder in Hollywood*, 321.
6. Quoted in Sinyard and Turner, *Journey Down Sunset Blvd.*, 161.
7. The last time the name came up in a Wilder film was as the title of a bar on a Mexican town set in *Hold Back the Dawn*. The sense of Climax as being on the edge of the real world and on the edge of fantasy is thus reinforced. The sense of it being, recalling *Double Indemnity*, a spiritual graveyard at the end of the world is also evoked.
8. Madsen, *Billy Wilder*, 138–142.
9. Quoted in Zolotow, *Billy Wilder in Hollywood*, 319–320.

Chapter 13

1. Wilder and Diamond, *The Fortune Cookie*, 158.
2. *Ibid.*, 120.
3. Quoted in Madsen, *Billy Wilder*, 143.
4. Wilder and Diamond, *The Fortune Cookie*, 119.
5. *Ibid.*, 123.
6. Farber, "The Films of Billy Wilder," 17.
7. Wilder and Diamond, *The Fortune Cookie*, 144.
8. Vincent Canby quoted in Baltake, *Jack Lemmon*, 167.
9. Wilder and Diamond, *The Fortune Cookie*, 141.
10. *Ibid.*, 132.
11. Quoted in Hunter, *Walter Matthau*, 70.
12. Quoted in Baltake, *Jack Lemmon*, 169.
13. So wittily catered to in that archetypal '60s Lemmon vehicle *How to Murder Your Wife* in 1965.
14. Wilder and Diamond, *The Fortune Cookie*, 142.
15. Wilder and Diamond, *The Apartment*, 73.
16. Hollis Alpert quoted in Dick, *Billy Wilder*, 91.
17. Wilder and Diamond, *The Fortune Cookie*, 162.
18. Zolotow, *Billy Wilder in Hollywood*, 309.
19. Wilder and Diamond, *The Fortune Cookie*, 131.
20. The irony is deliberate. It is obvious how we are meant to read the prospect of a man feigning a personal disaster and watching a real one. Of course, the real disaster in Harry's life is "fortune cookie" Sandy.
21. Nichols and Gassner, *Best Film Plays of 1945*, 121.
22. Wilder and Diamond, *The Fortune Cookie*, 168.
23. Farber, *The Films of Billy Wilder*, 10–11.
24. Keith Jackson's idiomatic commentary lends the film's opening an authenticity which is thoroughly consonant with Wilder's feeling for this staple American pastime.

Chapter 14

1. Originally filmed in 1931 and starring Adolphe Menjou as editor Walter Burns and Pat O'Brien as his protégé Hildy Johnson.
2. The only seam which shows is a brief impersonation by Hildy of James Cagney. Set as the '20s were turning into the '30s, this is inaccurate as Cagney didn't emerge as a recognizable star image until 1931's *The Public Enemy*.
3. The negligence victim cited by "Whiplash Willie" in his speech to the lawyers in *The Fortune Cookie*.
4. Quoted in Hunter, *Walter Matthau*, 126.
5. Wilder quoted in D'Arcy, "Making the Front Page the Wilder Way," 218.
6. Brown, "The Front Page," 32.

Chapter 15

1. Baltake, *Jack Lemmon*, 255.
2. Diamond quoted in Turner, "Interview with I. A. L. Diamond," 21.
3. *Ibid.*, 21.
4. Quoted in Kakutani, *The Poet at the Piano*, 8.
5. Itself a meticulously constructed mock–Spanish facade especially built for the film.

Bibliography

Books

Agee, James. *Agee on Film* (Volume 1). New York: McDowell-Obolensky, 1958.

Anderson, Janice. *Marilyn Monroe*. London: Hamlyn, 1983.

Anobile, Richard J., ed. *Ernst Lubitsch's Ninotchka*. New York: Flare/Darien House, 1975.

Baltake, Joe. *Jack Lemmon, His Films and Career*. London: Columbus, 1987.

Baxter, John. *Hollywood in the Thirties*. London: Zwemmer, 1968.

Bordwell, David, Janet Staiger and Kristin Thompson. *The Classical Hollywood Cinema: Film Style and Mode of Production to 1960*. London: Routledge, 1988.

Bullock, Alan, and Oliver Stallybrass, eds. *Fontana Dictionary of Modern Thought*. London: Fontana, 1977.

Corliss, Richard. *Talking Pictures—Screenwriters in the American Cinema*. Woodstock: Overlook Press, 1985.

Crowther, Bosley. *The Great Films: 50 Golden Years of Motion Pictures*. New York: G. P. Putnam's Sons, 1967.

Dick, Bernard F. *Anatomy of Film*. New York: St. Martin's Press, 1990.

_____. *Billy Wilder*. New York: Da Capo, 1996.

Dickens, Homer. *The Films of Barbara Stanwyck*. Secaucus: Citadel Press, 1984.

_____. *The Films of Ginger Rogers*. Secaucus: Citadel Press, 1975.

Eyles, Allen. *James Stewart*. London: W. H. Allen, 1984.

Freedland, Michael. *Jack Lemmon*. London: Weidenfeld and Nicholson, 1985.

Froug, William. *The Screenwriter Looks at the Screenwriter*. London: Macmillan, 1972.

Giannetti, Louis. *Masters of the American Cinema*. Englewood Cliffs: Prentice-Hall, 1981.

Halliwell, Leslie. *Halliwell's Film Guide*. London: Paladin, 1988.

Higham, Charles, and Joel Greenberg. *The Celluloid Muse: Hollywood Directors Speak*. London: Angus and Robertson, 1969.

_____. *Hollywood in the Forties*. London: Zwemmer, 1968.

Holtzman, Will. *William Holden*. New York: Pyramid Press, 1976.

Hunter, Allan. *Walter Matthau*. London: W.H. Allen, 1984.

Jackson, Charles. *The Lost Weekend*. London: Penguin Books, 1989.

Kakutani, Michiko. *The Poet at the Piano*. New York: Times Books, 1982.

Kanin, Garson. *Hollywood*. New York: Hart-Davis MacGibbon, 1975.

Kaplan, E. Ann, ed. *Women in Film Noir*. London: British Film Institute, 1978.

Konigsberg, Ira. *The Complete Film Dictionary*. London: Bloomsbury, 1988.

Lindbergh, Charles A. *Autobiography of Values*. New York: Harcourt Brace Jovanovich, 1976.

McBride, Joseph, ed. *Film-Makers on Film-Making* (Volume 1). Los Angeles: J. P. Tarcher, 1983.

McCann, Graham. *Marilyn Monroe*. Cambridge: Polity/Basil Blackwell, 1988.

McShane, Frank. *The Life of Raymond Chandler*. New York: E. P. Dutton, 1976.

Madsen, Axel. *Billy Wilder*. London: Secker and Warburg, 1968.

Manvell, Roger, ed. *The International Encyclopedia of Film*. London: Rainbird/Michael Joseph, 1972.

Mast, Gerald. *The Comic Mind*. Chicago: University of Chicago Press, 1973.

Nichols, Dudley, and John Gassner, eds. *Best Film Plays of 1945*. New York: Crown, 1945.

Poague, Leland A. *The Hollywood Professionals* (Volume 7). London: Zwemmer, 1976.

Quinlan, David. *Illustrated Directory of Film Stars*. London: Macmillan, 1992.

Quirk, Lawrence J. *The Films of William Holden*. Secaucus: Citadel Press, 1973.

Ricci, Mark, and Mark Conway. *The Complete Films of Marilyn Monroe*. Secaucus: Citadel Press, 1964.

Sarris, Andrew. *The American Cinema: Directors and Directions 1929–1968*. New York: E. P. Dutton, 1968.

Schickel, Richard. *Double Indemnity*. London: British Film Institute, 1992.

Sedgwick, Michael. *Passenger Cars 1924–1942*. London: Blandford Press, 1975.

Seidman, Steve. *Billy Wilder*. London: G. K. Hall & Co., 1977.

Sinyard, Neil, and Adrian Turner. *Journey Down Sunset Blvd*. Ryde: BCW Publishing, 1979.

Thomas, Bob. *The Films of Kirk Douglas*. Secaucus: Citadel Press, 1991.

Thomson, David. *A Biographical Dictionary of the Cinema*. London: André Deutsch, 1994.

Tuska, Jon. *Close-Up: Hollywood Director*. Metuchen: Scarecrow Press, 1978.

Tyler, Parker. *Magic and Myth of the Movies*. London: Secker and Warburg, 1971.

Vizzard, Jack. *See No Evil*. New York: Simon and Schuster, 1970.

Wernblad, Annette. *Brooklyn Is Not Expanding*. London: Associated University Presses, 1992.

Wilder, Billy, and I. A. L. Diamond. *The Apartment* and *The Fortune Cookie*. London: Studio Vista, 1966.

Wood, Tom. *The Bright Side of Billy Wilder, Primarily*. Garden City: Doubleday, 1970.

Zolotow, Maurice. *Billy Wilder in Hollywood*. New York: G. P. Putnam's Sons, 1977.

Articles

"Ace in the Hole." *Today's Cinema* (3 March 1951): 6.

"Ace in the Hole." *Monthly Film Bulletin* (April, 1951): 242.

"Ace in the Hole." *Observer* (17 June 1951).

Adair, Gilbert. "Wilder Bewildered," *Sight and Sound*. (Winter, 1976–77): 52–53.

Agee, James. "Sunset Boulevard." *Sight and Sound* (November, 1950): 283–285.

Allyn, John. "Double Indemnity: A Policy That Paid off." *Literature/Film Quarterly* (Spring, 1978): 116–124.

"Ball of Fire." A 1942 press release on vernacular used in the film. Available at the British Film Institute Reading Room.

"Ball of Fire." *Monthly Film Bulletin* (March, 1942): 30.

[Billy Wilder's credits.] *Film Comment* (Winter, 1970-71): 112.

Brown, Geoff. "The Front Page." *Monthly Film Bulletin* (February, 1975): 32–33.

Brunette, Peter and Gerald Peary. "Tough Guy — James M. Cain Interviewed." *Film Comment* (May-June, 1976): 50–57.

Combs, Richard. "Buddy Buddy." *Monthly Film Bulletin* (January, 1982): 4–5.

Comerford, Adelaide. "Kiss Me, Stupid." *Films in Review* (February, 1965): 118.

Crowther, Bosley. "'Double Indemnity,' a Tough Melodrama, with Stanwyck and MacMurray as Killers, Opens at the Paramount." *New York Times* (11 September 1944).

Cunningham, E. A. "The Major and the Minor." *Motion Picture Herald* (29 August 1942).

Cutts, John. "The Apartment." *Films and Filming* (September, 1960): 21–22.

D'Arcy, Susan. "Making the Front Page the Wilder Way." *Films Illustrated* (February, 1975): 216–218.

Diamond, I. A. L., and Billy Wilder. "Who Needs Writers?" and "Seeing in the Dark." From the 14th American Film Institute Life Achievement Award Programme (6 March, 1986).

"Double Indemnity." Press release from Paramount Pictures. Available at the British Film Institute Reading Room.

"Double Indemnity." *Monthly Film Bulletin* (August, 1944): 89.

Durgnat, Raymond. "Kiss Me, Stupid." *Films and Filming* (April, 1965): 27.

Dyer, Peter John. "The Apartment." *Monthly Film Bulletin* (August, 1960): 107.

_____. "Psycho and the Apartment." *Sight and Sound* (Autumn, 1960): 195–196.

_____. "Some Like It Hot." *Sight and Sound* (Summer-Autumn, 1959): 173.

Erens, Patricia. "'Sunset Boulevard': A Morphological Analysis." *Film Reader* (January, 1977): 90–95.

Eyquem, Olivier. "The Major and the Minor — Prelude et Fugue." *Positif* (July-August, 1986): 105–106.

Farber, Stephen. "The Films of Billy Wilder." *Film Comment* (Winter, 1971-72): 8–22.

Fenwick, J. H. "Kiss Me, Stupid." *Sight and Sound* (Spring, 1965).

Fitzpatrick, Ellen. "Some Like It Hot." *Films in Review* (April, 1959): 240–241.

"The Front Page." *International Photographer* (July, 1974): 13 and 18.

Gallagher, Brian. "'I Love You Too': Sexual Warfare and Homoeroticism in Billy Wilder's Double Indemnity." *Literature/Film Quarterly* (1987): 237–246.

Gillett, John. "The Spirit of St. Louis." *Sight and Sound* (Summer, 1957): 38–39.

_____. "Wilder's World." John Player Celebrity Series, National Film Theatre (15 March, 1970).

Gow, Gordon. "The Front Page." *Films and Filming* (March, 1975): 37.

Greenfield, Pierre. "Out of the Past." *Movietone News* (20 June, 1977): 40.

Griffith, Richard. "Biographical Notes on Billy Wilder." *Film Comment* (Summer, 1965): 63.

Guibert, Herve. "Le Mort Qui Parle — A Propos de 'Sunset Boulevard.'" *Cahiers du Cinéma* (January, 1981): 36–39.

Gunton, Sharon, ed. "Billy Wilder 1906–   ." *Contemporary Literary Criticism.* Volume 20 (1983): 455–466.

Hart, Henry. "The Spirit of St. Louis." *Films in Review* (March, 1957): 126–128.

Hersant, Yves. "Portrait de la Star en Singe Mort." *Positif* (September, 1983): 34–36.

Higham, Charles. "Cast a Cold Eye: The Films of Billy Wilder." *Sight and Sound* (Spring, 1963): 83–103.

_____. "Meet Whiplash Wilder." *Sight and Sound* (Winter, 1967-68): 21–23.

"Hold Back the Dawn." *Motion Picture Herald* (2 August 1941): 35.

"Hold Back the Dawn." *Monthly Film Bulletin* (October, 1941): 133.

Houston, Penelope. "Ace in the Hole." *Sight and Sound* (June, 1951): 45.

_____. "Scripting." *Sight and Sound* (January, 1951): 376.

Jeavons, Clyde. "The Front Page." *Sight and Sound* (Spring, 1975): 124.

Kann, Red. "The Lost Weekend." *Motion Picture Herald* (18 August 1945): 25.

"Kiss Me, Stupid." A 1965 press release detailing credits and synopsis. Available at the British Film Institute Reading room.

"Kiss Me, Stupid." *Monthly Film Bulletin* (March, 1965): 34.

"The Language Issue: The Front Page." *Journal of Film and Video* (Fall, 1996): 51–52.

Lemmon, Jack. "Such Fun to Be Funny." *Films and Filming* (September, 1960): 7.

Lightman, Herb. "Old Master, New Tricks." *American Cinematographer* (September, 1950): 309–320.

Lippe, Richard. "Kiss Me, Stupid — A Comedy Dilemma." *Velvet Light Trap* (Winter, 1971-72): 33–35.

"The Lost Weekend." *Monthly Film Bulletin* (September, 1945): 121.

"The Lost Weekend." *Today's Cinema* (25 September 1945): 10.

Luft, Herbert G., and Charles Brackett. "Two Views of a Director — Billy Wilder." *Quarterly of Film, Radio and TV* (Autumn, 1952): 58–69.

McBride, Joseph. "The Front Page." *Sight and Sound* (Autumn, 1974): 212.

_____, and Todd McCarthy. "Going for Extra Innings." *Film Comment* (January-February, 1979): 40–48.

_____, and Michael Wilmington. "The Private Life of Billy Wilder." *Film Quarterly* (Summer, 1970): 2–9.

McCourt, James. "Billy Wilder." *Framework* (Winter, 1976-77): 18–21.

McVay, Douglas. "Buddy Buddy." *Films and Filming* (June, 1982): 36–37.

"The Major and the Minor." *Monthly Film Bulletin* (December, 1942): 158.

Marple, B. G. "Ace in the Hole." *Films in Review* (August-September, 1951): 38–39.

Millar, Jeff. "The Front Page." *Film Heritage* (Spring, 1975): 35.

Milne, Tom. "Meet Whiplash Willie." *Monthly Film Bulletin* (July, 1967); 103–104.

Morris, George. "The Private Films of Billy Wilder." *Film Comment* (January-February, 1979): 33–39.

Mundy, Robert. "Wilder Reappraised." *Cinema* (October, 1969): 14–22.

Naremore, James. "Making and Remaking Double Indemnity." *Film Comment* (January-February, 1996): 23–31.

Norman, Barry. Commentary on Wilder on the occasion of the BBC airing of an *Arena* documentary on Wilder and some Wilder films. *Radio Times* (18–24 January 1992): 26.

Onosko, Tim. "Billy Wilder." *Velvet Light Trap* (Winter, 1971-72): 29–32.

Phillips, Gene D. "Billy Wilder." *Literature/Film Quarterly* (Winter, 1976): 3–11.

Poague, Leland A. "The Politics of Perception: Wilder's 'Stalag 17.'" *Film Criticism* (Winter, 1976-77): 19–25.

Prigozy, Ruth. "Double Indemnity: Billy Wilder's Crime and Punishment." *Literature/Film Quarterly* (1984): 160–170.

Programme Notes for *Double Indemnity* screening at the Museum of the Moving Image (June, 1989).

Robinson, David. "Some Like It Hot." *The Times* (20 May 1959).

Rowan, Arthur. "Making the Aerial Shots for 'The Spirit of St. Louis.'" *American Cinematographer* (June, 1957): 366–387.

Sarris, Andrew. "Billy Wilder: Closet Romanticist." *Film Comment* (July-August, 1976): 7–9.

_____. "Why Billy Wilder Belongs in the Pantheon." *Film Comment* (July-August, 1991).

"The Seven Year Itch." *Today's Cinema* (28 July 1955): 7.

"The Seven Year Itch." *Monthly Film Bulletin* (September, 1955): 138.

Sinyard, Neil, and Adrian Turner. Programme Notes for the Wilder and "Corridors of Paranoia" seasons at the National Film Theatre (December, 1979 and August, 1980).

"Some Like It Hot." *Monthly Film Bulletin* (June, 1959): 69.

"Some Like It Hot." *Films and Filming* (June, 1959): 23–24.

Spiller, David. "A World of Wilder." *London Magazine* (June, 1968): 76–82.

"The Spirit of St. Louis." *Today's Cinema* (28 May 1957): 10.

"The Spirit of St. Louis." *Monthly Film Bulletin* (July, 1957): 85.

"Stalag 17." *Monthly Film Bulletin* (July, 1953): 103.

Stevens, John D. "The Unfading Image from the Front Page." *Film and History* (December, 1985): 87–89.

"Sunset Boulevard." *Monthly Film Bulletin* (September, 1950): 137.

Taylor, John Russell. "Meet Whiplash Willie." *Sight and Sound* (Summer, 1967): 147–48.

Traubner, Richard. "Retrospectives in Berlin." *Films in Review* (August-September, 1980): 419–421.

Turner, Adrian. "Interview with I. A. L. Diamond." *Films and Filming* (May, 1982): 16–21.

_____, and Neil Sinyard. "Buddy Buddy." *Positif* (July-August-September, 1983): 47–49.

Tynan, Kenneth. "Climax Disaster." *Observer* (28 February 1965).

Walker, Michael A. "Billy Wilder." (A review of Axel Madsen's book). *Screen* (March-April, 1969): 103–108.

Young, Colin. "The Old Dependables." *Film Quarterly* (Autumn, 1959): 2–7.

Index

ADY-0779

WITHDRAWN